A Process
Called Conversion

A Process Called Conversion

DAVID K. O'ROURKE, O.P.

Doubleday & Company, Inc.
Garden City, New York
1985

Library of Congress Cataloging in Publication Data

O'Rourke, David K.
A process called conversion.
1. Conversion. 2. O'Rourke, David K. 3. Catholic
Church. Ordo initiationis christianae adultorum.
4. Catholic Church—Liturgy. I. Title.
BR110.O76 1985 248.2'4
ISBN 0-385-19636-9
Library of Congress Catalog Card Number 84-18691

CONTENTS

INTRODUCTION

We were called the silent generation. We found our voices late because the words of gratitude come less readily than cries of rage. The middle fifties were a time of peace. And we were confident and hopeful. That there was a monster being bred for our undoing in Indochina we did not know. That we lived alongside a resentment as old as the slave markets of the South and as inflammable as the wooden slums of Newark and Detroit we dared not suspect.

Mere children during the Depression, we watched the newsreels of the war impressed with the confidence that was the government's public policy. We came into adulthood knowing that evils could be tamed by human effort and believing that our efforts, properly formed, could do the taming. In a time of opportunity like ours, when military uniforms meant weekly drills and summer cruises, it was only the cynic who raised his voice. Heirs of the Western world, we lived convinced that our patrimony was permanent.

For many of my friends the Church was a wellspring of this heritage, albeit fouled by the earthiness of American Catholicism. But in those years they looked confidently for the good days that were to come. Then, they told me, a renewed Church of art and intellect and true spirituality would emerge to renew an institution mired in kitsch and conformity.

In the spring of my senior year I was asked by Catholic friends to join them for a weekend retreat at a Trappist monastery. I did not know what a retreat was. I had never seen a monastery. Yet I decided to go along. I suspect that the appeal of a few days in the country, away from New Haven's gray and still wintry bleakness, and in the company of the friends who would all soon go their own ways, was the reason I decided to go.

As we drove north into the Connecticut hills and then to Massachusetts' rolling, rural farmlands we found that the spring thaw was more advanced than along the coast. The sun was moving overhead from its winter's course on the horizon, and it was already warm and bright. Buds had begun to swell, giving the silver gray of the barren trees a deep red cast. Already the roadside grasses were showing green under the taller and breaking stalks of last year's growth. Looking at the coming of spring in these rolling hills I never once anticipated how pivotal this weekend and this spring would be in my life.

My side window musings ended abruptly when we pulled up, incongruously it seemed, at the front door of a prosperous dairy farmhouse. The door was opened by a monk in a white canvas tunic surmounted with a black hood. He counted us with his eyes, assuring himself that the five of us had come. Then he showed us to a stable now converted to a dormitory for visiting college students. He was running late and seemed impatient with our desire to wander off. After a rapid rundown of blankets, linens, and showers he moved toward the door. Vespers, he said, would be in twenty minutes.

Good, I thought, it will soon be time for vespers. After my first view of the dairy, the farmhouse, the converted stable, and this businesslike monk whose dress seemed so affected in this setting, it was good to hear mention of something that sounded monastic. Then I wondered what vespers were.

Over the brow of the hill, and hidden from the view of the farmhouse, lay the monastery's low stone buildings. Gray-brown fieldstone walls supported broad slate roofs. They seemed examples of studied simplicity, combining the directness of modern lines with the classicism of Roman arches.

The abbey church was imposing, and our path across the shoulder of the concealing hill showed it at its most imposing, especially the long sweep of roof that stretched from the low walls up to a high peak. Bells were ringing as we followed our guide, still impatient and still running late, along the unpaved farm road to the church. I expected to be led to the front door of the church, but our approach revealed that the front opened into a courtyard walled in by a square of abbey buildings. We were led instead to a small door opening into the right transept of the cruciform church. We entered into a narrow, stone-walled chamber separated from the body of the church by a heavy iron grille.

The grille was so placed that we could not see the monks, whose chanting we soon heard, nor could they see us. Two women, kneeling in front of the grille, further blocked our view. They were, I assumed, the owners of the Jaguar and the wood-paneled station wagon parked alongside the unpaved road. In the darkness of the church, dimly lighted by the setting March sun, I could make out the impressive expanse of roof but very little beneath it.

I began to sit down on what proved to be a very uncomfortable straight-backed wood-and-rush chair. However, I noticed that my friends were all kneeling and were using the rush-covered bench that jutted from the back of the chair in front of each one. I tried to kneel as they were, but the little bench was too high for comfort. The edge and the rush cut into my knees, so I sat again, not knowing what to expect next.

My impressions to that point were no preparation for what I would experience. The prosperous farm with its imposing guesthouse; the new stone buildings attempting to combine simple, modern elegance with monastic tradition, and obviously done at great cost; the two women in winter tweed, one with a silk scarf covering her head, the other wearing a black lace mantilla—they all bespoke the kind of worldly and image-conscious church which I knew so well and which interested me so little.

After sitting as far back in my chair as its discomfort would allow I was startled to see a moving flame light the dark just in front of the grille. Then I saw that it was part of a candlelighter carried by a monk in his early twenties. The youthfulness of his face was accentuated by his shaved head. The tonsure looked so inappropriate, even unnatural, on a man as young as I.

He lighted six tall candles in the semidarkness in front of the grille, revealing a rectangular, utterly simple stone altar. Then he circled back in front of the grille. As he passed he gave a quick and furtive glance at the small group of outsiders. The intensity of that glance fed my growing sense that there were radically different worlds on either side of that grille.

As soon as the candlelighter disappeared a feeble voice—that of the aged abbot, I was told later—began chanting in Latin. The chant was taken up by a contrastingly strong-voiced, large community. Then the abbot, bending under the weight of the heavy cope he was wearing, moved to the altar and into our view. He was accompanied by three young men. With the help of his assistants he began incensing the altar, walking around it as he did so. The grille partially obscured my view, but I could follow their progress by the clanking of the censer's chains and the puffs of yellow smoke that rose into the air.

As the abbot returned to the center of the altar the lesser of the three assistants knelt before him and received a large morocco volume from the first assistant. The kneeling man rested the top of the open book against his forehead, the bottom on his outstretched palms. With this human bookstand before him the abbot chanted a short prayer, there was a brief response from the unseen monks, the book was closed, the bookstand stood up, and the abbot and his assistants disappeared from view. The same intense young man returned, but with his head firmly lowered he succeeded in keeping his eyes within the grille and snuffed out the candles. The kneeling women crossed themselves, stood, and slipped out the door. I was alone and in silence.

I was not quite sure what it was I had seen. But I was beginning to have the unsettling feeling that for the first time in my life I was seeing people whom I judged to be not all that different from me take religion seriously.

For the remainder of the weekend, despite the dinner conversations with the other retreatants, and despite the late-night bantering with my friends in our stable, my mind kept coming back to the same idea: these men really believe what they are doing. They had turned their backs on the world, even on the world of the Church, for a hidden life of prayer. Their silence was broken only for the chanting of their prayers. The absoluteness of their renunciation ran counter to everything I believed and I found myself shaken by this unexpected and unwelcome challenge to my own values.

I returned to my studies, but the image of absolute commitment so integral to that life remained with me. A few nights later one of my companions at the monastery revealed his own similar reaction. Like me he was preparing for a law career, and like me he was disconcerted by the lived belief that there are more important things in life than control and affluence. Religion, we were prepared to admit, had real social and personal value. The Church had an inner logic that was compelling. And having grown up in a still anti-Catholic era we were prepared to defend one of the Church's most valued traditions—monasteries and the monastic life.

But what we had seen was different. We had not encountered monasteries as an idea. We had seen monks, some as young as we, living a life of the meanest form of manual labor, sleeping in dormitories with no privacy, in a life with no prospect of advancement, personal glory, or even the least bit of mobility, and vowed to this life for all their days.

As the hour grew late and our bottle of scotch empty, we concluded that the monastic life was not as much compelling as bizarre. Such total effacement was akin to suicide, and for what purpose? Social usefulness and religious values could be maintained in the Church at a much lower price than we had seen. The experience, we concluded, was unsettling. But then so are most exposures to an aberrant life.

Our senior year was a time for making plans. Graduate programs had to be laid out and schools chosen. Then came the applications for medical school, law school, and graduate programs in the humanities. We approached our faculty friends for letters of recommendation hoping that a good word from an eminent scholar might tip the scales in our favor. And we filed applications for the fellowships we hoped would make the studies less pressured.

Our futures were as public as our lives together. We debated the merits of the different graduate schools and the value or futility in trying to prepare for the graduate records exam or the legal and medical aptitude tests until the small hours of the morning. With each other we went through the excitement of making plans, the fears of rejection, the relief that came with a letter of acceptance and the celebration that followed upon it.

Those planning European studies had the luxury of making what we jokingly called appropriately aristocratic plans, little realizing how accurate we were. Was it best to land at Cherbourg or Le Havre? Which routes were best to take south before returning to Paris, London, or the English university towns before classes began?

I had decided to go to law school. But after my experience at the monastery the pleasure of anticipation had gone out of my plans. My application went off to Columbia Law School, and the acceptance came back bringing with it none of the sense of accomplishment that should have been there.

And then, out of nowhere but with a compelling clarity, came a realization. "I am not going to law school." I cannot describe this as a decision. One part of my mind, unbidden it seemed, presented this conclusion and I simply acquiesced. With the acquiescence came a great sense of relief. It was as though a terrible and joyless duty had been lifted from me.

How can I account for this reaction? This is a book about conversion, and I imagine it is obvious that I am describing the beginnings of my own conversion. But conversions do not occur in the abstract. Conversion literally means a turning, and it is people who turn. So this book is about the turnings in our lives. I want to describe the process of conversion because I believe that few moments are as powerful and mobilizing as our moments of conversion. We can benefit from them so much more when we recognize them for the wellsprings of creativity that they are.

As I noted, I am beginning by speaking of my own experience. But none of us turns only to something. We all come from somewhere. The turning involves a direction from which we turn, and it requires some compelling reasons to bring us to make that turn. What were the reasons at play in my life?

Earlier I mentioned my plans to study law. These plans were in response to my family's expectations that we would all do well. Following their years in the war my four older brothers were setting out on professional and business careers. They and my cousins, like their parents before them, would do well. It was a quiet and simple assumption, something not spoken as much as taken for granted.

Doing well did not necessarily mean becoming rich. That was quite secondary. It meant excelling. Anyone could be part of the crowd and could follow the crowd's rules. And anyone could be ordinary. We, on the other hand, were told that we could be different. We were expected to excel.

Excellence brought its rewards. It meant self-respect, and it meant the respect of one another. Excellence did not necessarily require power, but it did include freedom from the frustrations and indignities that beset the rest of humankind. Most people, it was pointed out, talked about things and other people. But excellence presupposed the development of an intellectual life, the ability to look critically at life and the world, and the means to talk about ideas.

Excellence also demanded its price. It required that you work to become the master of your environment, which took discipline and determination. It required that you look at the earthiness of ordinary people with a certain tolerance, perhaps even an amused affection, but also with the realization that that earthiness could lead you from more important goals.

This description now sounds to me more like the Stoic values of the ancient Romans than those of a Catholic family. But the rituals of our religion did not need to trespass into the field of the principles we lived by. To these Stoic values I added my own priorities. Stoicism in the life of an adolescent pressured to do well can become manipulative and self-centered. I was no exception. The critical transformation from self-interest to the morality that comes only upon experiencing the worth of others I had yet to realize. Cleverness and the bending of rules was not yet a matter of morals. For me at that time it was simply a matter of method.

In my last year in college I began to recognize this fundamental moral inadequacy. Several incidents stand out in my memory with a clarity that extends to the details of surroundings and dress. These incidents were all connected with the one moral issue that did manage to penetrate our comfortable world, the McCarthy investigations of the middle fifties.

I was a member of a university club whose sole purpose was to bring together small numbers of undergraduates and faculty. That that was the chief value of a university escaped me at the time. University education was already beginning its move from ethics to technology. But the year of the educational technologist had not yet come. We were practitioners of intellectual fencing and might have spent our energies in these effete games had we been left on our own. But we were not without the influence of wise men.

One afternoon I was introduced to a gracious and gentle young man, the guest of one of the club members. He turned out to be a high school senior out college-shopping. His camel-colored sweater, which almost matched the shade of his hair, and his khaki pants spoke of life in a college town.

We were talking about the McCarthy investigations and the question of Robert Oppenheimer's security clearance. Dr. Oppenheimer's loyalty was under attack in Congress and in the press. Since security clearance was required for work in government-sponsored atomic energy projects, and since the government was involved in almost all the projects, security clearance was almost a must for an atomic physicist.

Association with anyone denied that clearance could be politically and professionally dangerous.

The young man sat listening to us and then mentioned that his father worked with Dr. Oppenheimer in Princeton. Our social sense would have permitted him to shift the conversation from what might have become a personally uncomfortable discussion. Instead, with grace and intelligence, he defended the two scientists as well as the freedom necessary for their work.

Like my friends I was prepared to defend intellectual freedom from demagoguery, using a fashionable combination of reason and rancor. But this young man was not interested in our games. He was personally involved in this national scandal and was distressed by it. What for me was an interesting subject that never threatened my own self-interest was a painful reality to him.

He did more than defend the scientists. He made a personal appeal for us to respond with compassion to their plight. I was taken aback to find myself talking with someone, appreciably younger than I, who believed in the integrity of others and who had the courage to defend them publicly and before strangers.

The second incident, some weeks later, was almost a continuation of the first. In the same small room I was discussing the ongoing investigations with two friends. One of our teachers, Cleanth Brooks, a writer and critic, was seated in the corner near a window, reading by the light of the late afternoon sun. As the discussion progressed he lowered his journal and looked at us, from one to the other, obviously following our conversation. Apparently we reached one of those points where what is to be said has been said, and we fell silent. He leaned forward in his chair and asked us, very seriously, "Well, what are you going to do about it?" I must have appeared startled by his question, for he looked at me and repeated it: "What are you going to do about it?"

Where our conversation went at that point I do not remember. What I do recall is the challenge he set before us and, implicit in it, the belief that we were capable of doing something. That I could do something other than cope with the pressures facing me did not seem real. That I ought to do something more had never occurred to me. I was going about the business of having my wits sharpened and my mind educated so that I might better go about the pursuit of my own interests. Mr. Brooks left me with the suspicion that what I was doing was not only wrong but a waste of my own human ability, a suspicion that stayed with me.

A third incident helped push me further to the turning point. William Carlos Williams had been our family doctor and had seen me through my childhood ills. I had arranged for him to read his poetry at the university, and in the course of making the arrangements I had come to see him as a poet and intellectual, no longer as the family doctor.

He had been nominated for a national honor, but because of right-wing pressure the nomination was withdrawn. He was hurt by the withdrawal but also saddened to see people of supposed substance caving in before political pressure. He was discussing the nomination and withdrawal, and the enslaving effect that fear and prejudice can have in the life of an individual. Summing up his own reasons for advancing his ideas despite their unpopularity he quoted the scripture. "I remember being told when I was a young man that Jesus had said 'Know the truth, and the truth will make you free.' " I was chagrined to think that this man, a nonbeliever, should take the words of Jesus more seriously than did I, who, at least nominally, professed to believe them.

As our conversation continued his valuing of a mind freed from fear and prejudice stood out in contrast to my own self-serving pragmatism. He was wondering how honorable men could yield to the pressures of demagogues, a question I could answer quite easily. Recalling pictures of integrity pushed beyond its limits was painful for him. But the pain was his, not mine. Rather offhandedly I commented that these men were probably afraid, as though that fear not only explained but justified their actions. He was pensive for a moment, then spoke of something else.

Later I realized the rebuke implicit in that silence and in the change of subject. It was only implicit, and perhaps unthought. But it was real enough to make me begin to wonder whether my attitude to injustice would be so cavalier were I its victim.

I do not catalog these events to prove the moral immaturity of adolescence, nor to show how great men, or even a good young man, can influence the lives of the young. I write to explain conversion. We do not move to a conversion unless the inner voices of our own being impress on us a need to change. I recall these events because they impressed on me my own moral inadequacy, an inadequacy which I could no longer tolerate.

How these voices speak to others, and where the insistence comes from, will vary. The need to change can be forced upon us as though from the outside, by the circumstances in which we find ourselves. It may come on the heels of a dialogue within us. But in all these instances it seems to involve the realization that something has got to give. Things cannot keep going the way they are.

Conversion is not a magic moment. It is a human process. It is a process with moments and characteristics we can understand. The process may occur quickly or have the appearance of surprise, as in the conversion of St. Paul. It may occur over a long period of time, and we will see examples of a more progressive conversion. Often there are incidents that set the stage for the conversion, the way that the interactions I described above prepared me for the experience at the monastery. But whatever the situation I believe that the process of conversion can be understood.

After I had decided not to go on to law school I was faced with a basic question. What am I going to do now? Several years earlier the French philosopher Jacques Maritain had lectured on the philosophy of St. Thomas Aquinas. A friend who was a year ahead of me was influenced by Maritain and decided to pursue this study seriously. Maritain suggested that after graduation he study with the Dominicans at their House of Studies in the south of France. There, said the philosopher, a student would receive the best foundation available in Scholastic philosophy. So my friend, to the great surprise of his family, went off to live and study in a seven-hundred-year-old monastery set in the Provençal countryside so often painted by Cézanne.

We corresponded, and his letters to me described both the studies and the countryside. One of them came right at the time I decided to abandon my plans for law school. I wrote back asking him to arrange for me to do what he was doing, marveling as I did so at the incredible changes taking place in my life. I was informed, almost by return mail, that I was expected in this small, Provençal village in September.

What was happening to me, although I did not understand it at the time, was that I was undergoing a conversion. A weekend retreat brought into my life an aspect of human experience that was unknown to me. Questions were brought to the surface that were too real to be ignored. And in the attempt to answer them I quickly learned that my resources for answering them were inadequate. That inadequacy itself further deepened the sense of crisis in which I found myself.

So I called a halt to what I was doing. I declared a moratorium on future plans until I should have the means at my disposal to make those plans. I was going to go and live in Provence and catch up.

What I am describing here is the initial phases of conversion. Things in my life could not keep going the way they were. Something had to change. This pressure to change is an almost universal part of a conversion. We don't turn from the road we're on as long as it satisfies us. There has to be a lessening of that appeal, even real discomfort, before we move.

That discomfort may be on the surface and obvious to our own eyes, or it may be rumbling around more deeply within us. Both, I suspect, were true with me. The vocational choice and the pressure to fit into a study of law which I feared would be a dead end for me pushed me back from that study. But there was also, I suspect, a much deeper spiritual struggle that was brought near the surface by my experience in the monastery, although it took years to come fully into the open.

In this book I propose to look at the process of conversion. I will do so within the framework of the ancient rite used to receive converts into the Church. The rite has four stages, which account for the titles of our four sections. A conversion is principally a human story, and at the heart of this study are the stories of a few people, one especially, who underwent changes of direction, belief, and life itself. For better or worse one of these people kept track of her questions to me, notes of my answers, and a record of our conversations over a two-year period. To that cataloging this book is due.

A Process
Called Conversion

I

CONVERSION

". . . Though each convert finds God and the Church in his own way, there is much in my story which reflects the times and culture we live in, and so may be of some general interest. If this account can help others to understand the conversion process and so lead people closer to God my purpose will be accomplished."

FROM JULIE'S ACCOUNT
OF HER CONVERSION

JULIE'S STORY

An Account of My Conversion and Christian Formation

I come from a long line of atheists and was raised to believe that all phenomena in the universe could be explained in purely material and scientific terms. This world view was to me a lucid and self-evident one, which seemed intellectually well-supported, and I never saw any reason to doubt it. The atheists I know do not "reject" God, they simply believe that he is a myth. My family is Jewish. But while I was raised with a sense of Jewish identity we were not religiously practicing at all.

Though I was raised ideologically as an existentialist, believing there to be no absolute frame of reference for morality, in practice my parents had a strong sense of values and were deeply committed to trying to bring about social justice in our society. They made a conscious effort to communicate these values to me. I have found this to be the case with many atheists.

From the time I was a young child I felt an almost mystical love for animals and for the world of nature. My family used to take trips into the nearby deserts and mountains of Southern California, and my father bought land and built a cabin in the pine-forested San Jacinto Mountains. Here my feelings intensified and became what I can describe only as religious. By my middle childhood years I was experiencing a profound sense of sacredness in nature. Because I could not describe it to myself in any other way, I secretly called it the spirit, and this communion with the spirit became the most important thing to me, the hidden core of my life.

I remained firmly convinced, however, that this was a purely psychological reaction to the beauties of nature, and not the action of God. I postulated that since most people had mistakenly assumed an objective existence for things spiritual, there must be some sort of universal religious drive in humankind, in the same way that there are sex drives or other universal components in our psyches. I had been taught the usual atheist explanations that people use religion to provide answers to basic questions in a prescientific age, that they need God as an emotional crutch to allay fear and provide a sense of security, etc. However, these explanations always seemed inadequate to explain the depth and nature of the religious experience.

I never explained to myself why such a tenaciously universal yet seemingly purposeless drive should exist. Given my knowledge of evolution and my scientific curiosity perhaps I should have wondered more.

In any event this contradictory set of affairs, namely an atheist world view coupled with spiritual yearnings, did not pose any intellectual strain on my atheism. I simply accepted the spiritual side as a quirk in my personality. Meanwhile the spirit remained the central but hidden core of my life, up until the time of my conversion at the age of twenty-nine.

While I was convinced that the world's various religions were purely cultural, mythological, and psychological affairs, with no objective foundations, I was interested in studying them and read all I could. Interestingly, though I went to college in the 1960s and '70s, when many people were turning to Eastern religions, I never felt personally attracted to them. I did feel drawn to the ancient Greek mystery religions, especially the Demeter-Persephone cult of Eleusis, with its emphasis on the cycles of nature, fertility of the earth, and the theme of death and rebirth.

From an early age I was also attracted to Catholicism, starting, I think, when I read a book about nuns at the age of ten or eleven. This book had quite an effect on me, though I wasn't consciously aware of it at the time. Among other things, it reinforced in me a tendency toward rigorous self-examination, for which I'm grateful. Unfortunately, this particular convent also had a strong Jansenist flavor which gave me some rather warped views of Catholicism.

As I grew older and began to read and learn more about Catholicism, I was also drawn to the idea of the sacraments, especially the Eucharist. In part I was attracted by the depth of archetypal meaning in these simple, earthy symbols (recall my love for the Greek mystery religions), but also I think there were reasons whose roots lay deeper.

I wanted somehow to enter into and participate in this mystery. I sometimes read the Bible, and the year before my conversion I imposed a series of abstinences on myself during Lent. I went to the Easter vigil Mass, which deeply moved me.

I should make clear that I classed all of this as belonging to my emotional and imaginative life. My outlook remained strictly scientific and materialistic, and I used to argue vigorously with any friends who showed the slightest leanings toward religion, lest they fall into error. Many atheists feel a passionate commitment to The Truth and are pained at the prevalence of supposed religious "error" they see all around them. But looking back on this period now, I still believe that my approach to Christianity was largely an emotional one.

I want to describe something which in retrospect seems more important than it did at the time, namely the aversion I felt toward Catholicism. For while Catholicism among all of the present-day religions was the one that attracted me the most, I could have only short contacts with it before feeling the need to retreat. What made me pull back was a sense of unhealthy oppression or spiritual claustrophobia.

My personal "spirituality" was full of beauty, full of the fresh winds of a thunderstorm in the mountains, but it did not contain people. To me, morals and ethics, while important in my day-to-day life, seemed to be in a separate compartment, unrelated to this sacred spirit. I was disturbed by the centrally human element in all of the monotheistic religions, such as the concern with moral and historical elements, and in particular I had a hard time with the Catholic emphasis on sin and repentance.

I held the common stereotype of Catholics as being neurotically oppressed by guilt, denying the goodness of material creation, and especially any goodness in themselves. My perceptions came in part from certain Jansenist distortions of the church's spirituality which were more prevalent in the pre-Vatican II days when I was growing up.

Unfortunately, the few Catholics I knew as a child tended to confirm this image, and when I went to college most of the Catholics I knew were reluctant to talk about their faith. This was during the turbulent period following Vatican II.

There was also a more personal reason for my aversion to this aspect of Catholicism. I am a conscientious and self-observant person, and I think I unconsciously sensed that this Catholic emphasis on self-examination and the moral responsibility could lead, in a personality such as my own, to oppressive scrupulosity.

All this may sound as if I were on a spiritual search, shopping for a religion. It would sound even more so if I were to add that when I was in my mid-to-late twenties I occasionally went to Mass. I loved to draw out my religious friends on the subject of religion, not to argue but so that I could better understand what the heart of each religion or denomination was. However, as far as I was consciously able to discern, I felt no dissatisfaction with my atheism. I had long since accepted this side of myself as an anomaly which could be safely indulged.

My studies in college and graduate school were the natural sciences and psychology. I am deeply grateful for my background in the natural sciences. My family is artistic, and during those summers when I wasn't working or going to school I used to go into the San Jacinto Mountains to take ceramic classes. Pottery is a holy art, but I shall resist the temptation to elaborate on that point here.

When I first entered graduate school at the University of California at Berkeley I went through a relatively dormant period as far as spirituality goes. I was going through something of a culture shock, moving from the quiet forests of Santa Cruz, where I'd lived as an undergraduate, to the frenetic city of Berkeley. And besides this my graduate work absorbed most of my energy. Eventually I moved to an apartment in a quiet green area, with a bedroom window looking over a beautiful rambling garden. I was home again. So it was that shortly before Pope Paul VI died I began to experience a renewed internal flowering.

I reacted to the newspaper headlines announcing Pope Paul's death in a rather peculiar way for an atheist. That very day I went to the library and came home loaded with Catholic catechisms and books on the sacraments. Among these was Thomas Merton's *The Living Bread*, which has subsequently had a tremendous effect on my understanding of the Eucharist and the Mystical Body of Christ. I'd never heard of Thomas Merton before; I just pulled it off the shelf for its title.

When Pope John Paul I died so quickly after his election I was quite saddened and went to Mass the following Sunday as a memorial gesture. There, during the consecration and the Eucharistic prayer and communion rite which followed, I experienced an intense spiritual union with the people around me. For hours afterward I was filled with joy. I had never experienced this before, and though I didn't admit it to myself my atheism was a bit shaken. It seemed so profoundly real. I made an appointment to talk with the priest who'd said the Mass, to see whether he could account for what had happened, but later chickened out and canceled the appointment. Shortly after this I backed away from Catholicism because of an attack of the "spiritual claustrophobia" described earlier. Later I would tell my atheist friends that if I hadn't been such a convinced atheist this experience might have converted me. I prided myself on my objectivity and ability to distinguish merely psychological experiences from objective fact.

These attacks of skittishness seem to be common, and it can take a great deal of trust and patience for the religious person who is watching to know when to step back. To try to push a person forward at such times could be a great mistake, one which, fortunately, no one made with me.

The actual conversion itself, I now believe, was a direct act of God. While God had touched me many times and was already beginning to teach me a little about his ways I persisted in believing these glimpses could all be explained away. I will now describe the events leading to my conversion.

When I was in my twenties I was in love with a man who, like myself, was an atheist. We lived together for several years. A couple of years before my conversion a friend of his converted to a Christian fundamentalist sect, and he wanted to think of arguments to change his friend's mind. He began studying up on religion and, in particular, biblical historical and form criticism.

At this same time, for other reasons, I was experiencing a renewal in my own spiritual life. I intended to share these studies with him, but first I wanted to read the "original material," i.e., the four gospels. I was almost ashamed to admit that my real reason was not so much intellectual as that I felt a deep hunger to read and meditate on the gospel of Jesus Christ.

My friend would try out his anti-Christian arguments on me to see how effective they were. Because an argument is no fun if both people argue on the same side I played the Christian, using my small store of knowledge of Catholic theology. Soon we became intensely curious to know how an intelligent and educated Christian who knew his theology would answer some of the tough questions my friend proposed.

One day in early January 1979, I plucked up my courage and knocked on the door of the nearest Catholic church. I announced to the secretary that I was "nonreligious and have no desire to be converted but have some questions I'm intellectually curious about, if anyone can spare the time." Fortunately, the church I'd found was staffed by Dominicans who seemed interested in discussing my questions.

I'm sometimes tempted to think that God has a sense of humor, for he works through the strangest channels. In my case it was through the discussions with a fellow atheist bent on deconverting Christians that I met the priest who was later to instruct, guide, and baptize me.

It happened that the pastor was available, and we talked for an hour. I had expected to be intimidated by a priest. Instead, I felt as comfortable as though he had been a member of my own family. I was impressed with how intelligent, well reasoned, sensible, and humane his answers were. I could see that his mind was alive and in touch with worldly reality, and at the same time that he was grounded in a deep, solid, quiet spirituality. His replies were informed by centuries of Church teaching, and it intrigued me that the Church could think so reasonably. It was clear that he wasn't giving me his own private opinions or a modernized, watered-down compromise on Church teaching, and this impressed me favorably even though I didn't believe.

The healthy quality of his answers came as a pleasant surprise to me and contradicted all of my morbid stereotypes of Catholics. I left feeling happy that Catholics were in better shape than I'd thought and figured that that was the end of it. I didn't expect ever to see this priest again, and it was a full year before I was again knocking at the rectory door.

I should make it clear that at no time in this conversation or any of the subsequent meetings did he try to convert me or persuade me of the truth of his views. He simply answered my questions. I'm glad of this, for had he done otherwise I would have felt imposed upon and defensive, and my heart might have closed up.

A year later, just after New Year's Day in 1980, my atheist friend showed me a book on the Christian calendar which I bought and hungrily pored over. I found myself being fascinated with the season of Lent and was oddly touched by a Lenten penitential poem. With this my thoughts began to turn toward Christianity again, and I felt a desire to participate in the upcoming Lent in some way.

A strange thought began to haunt me, namely that I should make a confession to a Catholic priest concerning some things I'd done over ten years previously. These things were not connected with anything then current in my life, and in fact I considered them well behind me and had barely thought of them in the intervening ten years. This idea seemed totally inexplicable to me, as I believed in neither God nor the authority of the priesthood. I knew myself well enough to know it was not psychological counseling I desired. Nevertheless, I felt the need to make a confession, plain and simple. For some reason it seemed important to put these things behind me through this "official" symbolic act, and to make penitential reparation. I could think of no good reason to yield to this bizarre idea and resisted it for almost two weeks.

A few days before my conversion my friend and I attended the first of a series of meetings of informal dialogue between Jews and Christians. It was led by a rabbi, a Lutheran minister, and a Catholic priest. Here were Jews, Christians, converts to each side, and mixed marriages as well as a wide range of religious beliefs. Somehow this meeting of Jews and Christians telling their stories, openly discussing their perceptions of each other, and establishing a fellowship with one another opened a door of inner healing. The presence of converts especially moved me. It was as if something I'd always yearned for, the communion between Jews and Christians, was for the first time experienced as permissible and possible, and a lifelong, unspoken taboo was lifted. I was surprised by this reaction in myself, which took place on a deep, inarticulate level, as I'd not been aware of this yearning. An important door was opened that night, though at the time I didn't realize it.

A few days later I yielded to this persistent sense that I should confess, and phoned the pastor I had spoken with a year ago. It was a Friday, and I phoned him from my office. I very nervously told him that I wanted to see him. He remembered me from the year before. I couldn't tell him over the phone that it was to make a confession. He gave me an appointment for the next day, in the morning.

That evening I was in agony, alternately dreading the horrible prospect of making the confession and fearing that as I was not Catholic he would have to turn me away without hearing the confession at all. I was so nervous that I cleaned the entire apartment from top to bottom. I made an examination of conscience, using a guide in a catechism I'd recently bought. The odd thing is that I didn't make a general confession. The only thing I added as a result of this examination was a recent, fairly trivial incident—some unkind words spoken to a stranger. And though I could never have guessed it my conversion may have hinged on this little inclusion.

When I left my apartment on the morning of January 19, 1980, if someone had told me that in an hour from now I would believe in God I would have told them they were crazy. I expected to make the confession and then have everything return to normal. It was a dazzlingly fresh and sunny morning, after many days of rain.

I nervously explained to him what I was there for, adding that I knew I could not receive sacramental absolution, that I had not come for psychological counseling, and that I really didn't know why I was there. He agreed to hear the confession. It was difficult to do so, needless to say, and I will leave it at that. There was a certain penance which I offered to him which he accepted; this meant a lot to me.

After I had finished the confession he spoke briefly about God's mercy. He also spoke about the meaning of Christian humility, which is a very different thing from humiliation or debasement. With respect to the recent incident of unkindness, he told me that we can actually be thankful that we sometimes do wrongs which we cannot go back and repair, especially if we tend to pride ourselves on being "good" people. For such sins can remind us of our human limitations, and our need to turn to God and ask for his forgiveness, guidance, and strength. I think that somehow those simple words opened the final door in my heart, though I wasn't aware of it at that moment. At the end he said a prayer asking for God's forgiveness, and this seemed inexplicably precious to me. I was very grateful that he did that.

He made no attempt to convert me, but neither did he refrain from showing me his own faith in God. Much later, after my conversion, I asked him how he had been able to exercise this self-restraint when I was so clearly hanging in the balance. He told me it was because he trusted I was in God's hands.

I left then, feeling relieved and strangely moved. As I started to walk away I felt a desire to turn back, go into the church, and give thanks. I didn't stop to ask myself, "Give thanks to *whom?*" for I was used to these spiritual quirks in myself. I went inside the church, sat in one of the pews, and thought about what had happened. At this point I still had no idea that God had anything to do with it. But, unknown to me, the doors of my heart and mind now stood wide open.

Words can never describe what happened next. As I sat there I began to sense a presence which filled the entire church and also my entire being. It was the presence of love, of an all-knowing, all-wise, forgiving, and merciful God. I felt a profound peace, which emanated from all around me and within me and filled me. This communion was a quiet and gentle one. There was no mystical intensity, as I had sometimes experienced in the past, but a simple wholeness that surpasses words.

Somehow the very quietness of the awareness was part of what enabled me to recognize its source as real. My critical faculties were in no way suspended, and I found myself testing the presence and realizing, in astonishment, "This is no psychological experience coming from my mind, there is a real other here." Penetrated by and enveloped in this presence, I reflected on what had happened when I was making my confession, how this priest had truly been a human instrument through whom God's mercy had flowed. Even if I had never read about the theology of the priesthood—which I had—I think this would have been equally clear to me. I was profoundly grateful both to God and to this priest who had revealed God's love to me. His words and actions had been very simple, certainly unsentimental, yet they were a powerful sign and a living channel.

Before I go on to describe my subsequent journey I want to add a note for any skeptics who may be reading this. One could easily make a good case for explaining the conversion solely in terms of compensatory psychology. Very briefly, it would go like this. First, there is a long history of unfulfilled longings, experienced as spiritual desires. When I decide to make the confession, prompted by unconscious, unresolved guilt, I go through an intensely painful anticipatory anxiety experience. The confession is a cathartic experience, and in this vulnerable state I am treated kindly by the priest, a father figure. In consequence I experience a buoyant relief afterward, combined with gratitude and a cathexis of emotion to the priest, and mistake this complex of emotions for God.

I was acutely aware of this interpretation from the very start. As I have said, the conversion did not affect my ability to think critically, though this is commonly believed of new converts.

The time I spent sitting in the pew was short, perhaps fifteen or twenty minutes. But it turned my entire view of the universe upside down.

1

The Process of Conversion

In her narration Julie describes events that took place over a long period of time. She describes not just an event, but many events, and explains the connection between them. She is at pains to describe the process of her conversion. Process is a word I have used to describe conversion, and we think it important enough to have put it in the title. I will continue to speak of conversion not as an event, or a moment, but as a process. What does this mean?

A process is more complex and involving than a simple event or a moment in time. Process involves duration and continuity. It does not involve only an event, or a number of isolated events, but a series of related events played out over a period of time. Process, as I use the word here, includes not only the events but the people in the events. It involves all that they go through as they experience the events described.

Process involves time, change, and growth. These elements are explicitly recognized in the church's rite of initiation for adults, which envisages an entry process lasting about two years. During these two years much goes on in the life of the man or woman going through a conversion. Questions come to the surface, stresses are lived through, doubts are faced and resolved, and decisions are made. All these events, in all their complexity, are part of the process of conversion.

One of the important aspects of the church's process of initiating new members is that it is not explanatory. The rite does not attempt to explain what is going on. Rather it tries to guide and assist the people. The church's approach is social, it tries to help the individual go from the status of an outsider to that of a fully integrated member of a believing community.

This nonexplanatory approach is typical of Catholic liturgy. Liturgy is not self-reflective, not self-conscious. Rather it is symbolic, and symbolic actions are not explained, they are performed. They are performed not as much to educate as to transform.

This nonexplanatory approach notwithstanding, I, for one, prefer to understand what is going on. For me, portraying the process of conversion and initiation without a parallel explanation of motives and methods feels incomplete. Assuming that there are others like me, I will present an explanation of the process of conversion that parallels the rite itself. This explanation sees three phases in the process: an initial, noisy phase; a subsequent period of quiet and withdrawal; a final, more active and integrated phase.

Conversion, as I noted above, involves a turning from a path we are on to another. The incongruities of our present state build up to the point where they become intolerable. Questions suppressed, decisions postponed too long, realities ignored, items of personal agenda tabled once too often, whatever it may be, they mount up and bring us face-to-face with the realization that things have got to change.

This realization may manifest itself in boredom with the individual's work, or in a desire for new and different places, or in attraction to people or a way of living heretofore unacceptable. The young man or woman who leaves school to join a cult; the staid, seemingly unimaginative professor who runs off with a flamboyant young woman; the church official who lets go of a promising church career to throw himself directly into working with the poor and the marginal—these are all examples of conversion. The individuals could no longer abide their accustomed lives. Something had to give. What changed was their way of life.

This change can bring an overwhelming sense of relief, which often shows up as the noisy enthusiasm so typical of the new convert. With the resolution of stress and conflict, with anxiety about the future transformed into relief by the discovery that an alternative is not only possible but attractive, the relief can feel positively euphoric.

I recall the sense of euphoria that set in after I decided not to enter law school and, instead, to go to France to live. What was I going to do there? How would I live? Where would this all lead? I did not want to be bothered with these questions. They were asked by people who obviously did not understand. Things would work out. And I was as sure of this as I was happy in my choice.

This same euphoria can also be an excellent advertisement for a cult, a church, or a social movement. No testimonial is given with quite the enthusiasm, the conviction, and the air of happiness as that of a recent convert. It is no wonder that some millennial movements and religious groups routinely call on the recent convert to tell what the program, or the Lord, or the church has done for him. Recruiting sessions featuring the new convert have an ebullience and an energy that are typical of life when fear and doubt are transformed into the conviction that life could not be better.

There is a danger in placing too much importance on the convert's enthusiasm, a danger both for the individual and for the church. Enthusiasm, like all feelings, is transitory. It is an emotional overflow, a temporary side effect of the anxiety resolution that is such an important part of the first phase of conversion. It is a by-product of the conversion, not its essence. With time this euphoric enthusiasm is usually replaced by other emotions, usually much quieter and more inner-directed. But in groups where it is given a mystical or symbolic dimension this enthusiasm can be equated with all that is good in the conversion, or in the movement, or in the church. It can be seen as the principal good, to everyone's loss.

The damage comes from the understandable but nonetheless destructive tendency to exploit the enthusiasm. It is, as I mentioned, an unparalleled drawing card. Mark Twain gives us a classic and comic example of this in *Huckleberry Finn*. The Duke and Dauphin are discussing how to fleece a camp meeting. And with a professional's understanding of religion they decide on conversion. A repentant sinner, one decides, will make both tears and money flow. Better yet, suggests the other, a converted pirate. "Heathens don't amount to shucks alongside of pirates to work a camp meeting with."

For the very same reason any new convert will serve to attract people to his or her cause. But since the enthusiasm is an overflow from the sense of relief and euphoria, it will pass. And it should pass. Interiorizing the process of the conversion is aided by letting the noisy phase run its course. Unfortunately, it is common for people who are moving beyond the noisy phase to be thought of as backsliders. If the initial phase, because of its showiness, is seen as the whole process, then its loss will be equated with a loss of the conversion. But this is not true. The movement from the noisy phase into a quiet one is constructive.

Growth and maturity require interiorization. Change that is manifested in our emotions and typified by much external activity must become rooted in attitudes and beliefs if it is to endure. To go from emotions to values is part of a growth process, a building process, called interiorization. Put simply, it is a shifting of the area of conversion from the outside, or the externals, such as our enthusiasms, to the interior of our being, the beliefs and values we live by. And this requires time and quiet. Interiorization needs time to think things over, quiet and leisure to sort things out, the reflective setting that best suits our temperament and gives us the opportunity to make sense of what is happening to us. Commonly this process is advanced by having some distance from the turmoil and noise that often surround the beginning of a conversion. Like people who move into a new house and celebrate with their friends, they then need some time and quiet after all the partying in order to begin to appreciate what it is they now have.

Interestingly enough, we can see this in the life of St. Paul, himself. After his initial conversion on the road to Damascus there was a short period of somewhat frantic activity, during which he talked at length about what had happened to him. This was the noisy phase. But then he withdrew to Syria, where he lived quietly for several years. What he did during these years is not really known, but they were apparently quiet years. It was only after this period of quiet and anonymity that he began his journeying and writing, the apostolic work for which he is so well known.

This period of quiet and withdrawal, a time for making sense of what has happened, is followed by what we will call an integrated phase. What is integrated is the individual and the conversion. During the quiet time the changes have become one with the very personality of the convert. Now, the actions come not so much from an emotional overflow as from the individual's inner conviction. An expression of identity—"This is who and what I am"—replaces the euphoria—"Just listen to what has happened to me." This presupposes, of course, that there is more to the person than what has happened to him, a rather basic truth that sometimes dawns slowly on overactive people.

Psychologists maintain that the process of conversion is initially a situation of conflict resolution. This resolution, they say, can help in establishing life goals and firming up the values a person lives by. But for many people goals and values come only much later. They are part of a development that comes only after the first stage of conversion, a development that requires time and nurturing.

There is nothing essentially religious about the process of conversion itself. The process is a human one rooted in the dynamics of human life. Psychologists point out that an individual who is converted to evil manifests the same relief and euphoria as one converted to good. The person, for example, who is caught in between a pattern of behavior and a code of ethics that are irreconcilable, who finally gets to the point where something has got to give, and who resolves the conflict by surrendering his ethics and moving with abandon into his pattern of living may exhibit the very same relief and euphoria as one who surrenders the conflicted way of living in favor of his ethics.

Adolf Hitler's *Mein Kampf* is a biography of conversion, a conversion to evil. He was caught and immobilized by conflicting forces and resolved them by determining to move forcefully and wholeheartedly into a violent, racist and aggressive life. The book is an example of the noisy phase of conversion, and his life is an example of how a person can be trapped into a permanent exploitation of this phase.

There is also an interesting example of conversion away from the church in the letters of Flannery O'Connor. Her friend and correspondent, identified in her published letters only as "A," had become an unconvinced and uncomfortable Catholic. She eventually resolved this conflict by leaving the church. In response to a question about A's situation O'Connor wrote to another friend:

> I'll tell you what's with "A", why all the exhilaration. She has left the church. Those are the signs of release. She's high as a kite, and all on pure air. This conversion was achieved by Miss Iris Murdoch, as you could doubtless see by that paper. [She] now sees through everything and loves

everything and is a bundle of feelings of empathy for everything. She doesn't believe any longer that Christ is god and so she has found that he is "beautiful, beautiful!" Everything is in the eeeek, eeek, eureka stage. The effect of all this on me is pretty sick making, but I manage to keep my mouth shut. [Letter to Cecil Dawkins, January 10, 1962, *The Habit of Being* (New York: Vintage, 1980) p. 459.]

What is it that makes a conversion religious? Put simply, what the individual is converted to. Conversion becomes religious in the same way a man or woman can become religious, in virtue of what he or she is turning toward—God, the church, or a life of religious living.

The psychological view of conversion is descriptive. It outlines and explains the process. It does not attempt to evaluate it. A religious view of conversion, by contrast, is evaluative. It relates the process the person is going through to the faith, and uses the norms of the faith to guide and direct the process. The particular religious view of conversion we are using in this book is to be found in the church's rite of Christian initiation of adults. It is an encompassing view of how the individual goes about becoming a Christian and includes all the significant people and events that are part of the conversion process.

This rite of Christian initiation is especially useful to understand because of its importance in the church. In the Catholic Church theory does not give rise to practice. It is really the other way around. In the church the starting point for all theologies and theories is the community expressing its common faith at prayer. What the theologians and other theoreticians do is reflect on and schematize what the community believes and articulate that belief in a clear and logical manner.

An example of the community expressing its faith at prayer is to be found in this rite of Christian initiation. For it is during their common prayer that they open their community to new members. They do so in a ritualized way which is founded on the community's faith. This ritualized way is called a rite. In its reception of converts the church uses this ancient rite whose roots and shape go back to the first days of the Christian community. And this rite, with its four stages, is the basis for our explanation of the conversion process.

2

Coping with Change and Loss

The houses of my childhood, like the oaks and the traprock ridges, grew out of the earth and its permanence. They were the fixed base on which the changes of our life were acted out. They were part of what endured. Their destruction was a terrible violation of the set order of life.

I recall the fascination I experienced when, in violation of this order, an entire section of neighboring houses was condemned to be removed. They were in the way of a new road that was to come out from New York, cross through the miles of salt grass and marsh, burrow through our hills, and climb up and over the mountains to the west.

The houses were substantial. They stood in the shade of full-grown oak and elm trees, their heavy slate walks raised and canted by the spreading roots. The older houses, turreted Victorians with bay windows and covered porches, were too fragile to be moved. So they were torn down. Shorn of their roofs, stripped of their shingles, they were beaten into broken wood and plaster, shoveled into dented dump trucks, and driven away.

The newer houses, built right after the world war, were more tightly knit in virtue of the rectangularity then in fashion. They were compact

enough to be moved. Square-cut timbers, longer than the houses themselves, were pierced through their foundations. Jacks lifted the houses
above the foundations, and the supporting timbers were fitted with
wheels.

Harried workmen, semiemployables unhired by the war industries,
tramped through the rhododendrons and azaleas to the commands of a
martinet foreman. "Get those jacks level. Line up the wheels. Come
on, I want those wheels set now." Inch by inch the houses slid forward,
away from their foundations, shearing off the holly and forsythia and
lilacs that had grown with the families and decorated their festivals.

Large trucks towed them slowly and carefully away. Then, a half
mile away, they were crowded side by side on flat, naked, leftover
building lots where broken bottles lay among the trampled weeds.
Once surrounded by carefully kept gardens, they were now set off by
the mounds of red clay left by the basement excavators and the gray
puddles of cement water made by the masons.

Men and women whose sense of self had solidified in the homes they
established, who proved their endurance as they held on to what was
theirs during the Depression, and who then had their fears honed fine
in a way that could never happen again as they watched their sons go
off to war, stood by as their houses were taken from them. They could
have followed their houses to the treeless and littered fields. But, every
one, they moved far away from this scene of their violation.

And then their neighbors and friends, the rest of us, who with them
sensed fear when it was first announced that the road was coming, and
whose eyes brimmed with tears as the dispossessed shook hands, closed
the doors of their Buicks and DeSotos, and pulled away from the curb
for the last time—we fell like locusts on what they left behind. We
pried loose the bricks from the sheared-off chimneys, cleaned them of
their mortar, and piled them in neat stacks behind our houses. "The
Caterpillar tractors are going to level it all anyway." Men who sat at
desks all day long and who did not even own work clothes used the iron
pipes abandoned in the foundations to pry the slate walks free from the
earth's fifty-year hold. "They're going to send in steam shovels to dig it
all up." Shrubs were pulled loose from the packed earth, their broken
roots still holding clumps of damp soil. "Maybe we can save them.
Besides, they're going to die anyway." We pillaged what we would

never use and stored what we did not want. But in the process the once intrusive and much feared road was becoming our road.

I watched as the land on which I grew up was scraped away and the bedrock beneath was drilled with holes. We gathered around the foreman as he removed the detonator from its oak box, pumped the handle several times to increase the charge, connected the wires leading to the dynamite sticks, and then, after pausing to allow us to be impressed with his importance, pushed the plunger. We took part in the building of the road. And then, one by one, but by our own choice, we all moved away from it.

I believe that the change of a conversion can separate us from the familiar as truly as the building of the road separated our friends from us and from their roots. True, the convert moves in response to forces from within and may not experience the sense of violation that comes when it is imposed from the outside. But the change is equally real. And the sense of loss can be equally painful. The man or woman going through a conversion should listen to these voices of loss and try to understand what they are saying.

Change involves loss, and loss brings pain. The change that is part of conversion can easily lead to pain. Yet what seems most typical of the convert is a sense not of loss but of euphoria and well-being. To understand the place of change in a conversion I think we have to look beyond the euphoria. The euphoria is transitory, and when it leaves the underlying sense of loss is still there.

This is not to say that the euphoria is unreal and its source somehow deceptive. Nothing could be further from the truth. The resolution of those feelings that lead to the conversion—feelings of being trapped and immobilized, caught at a fork in the road with no means to know which path to take, the awareness that things cannot continue going the way they are and that something has to change—the resolution of these feelings will bring relief. The amount of energy that goes into coping with this indecision is apparently such that its release is rather heady. The feelings of well-being that come with knowing what you want to do and can do following upon a period of painful indecision are very real. So the euphoria of conversion is real, indeed.

In September 1955 I sailed for France on the *Queen Elizabeth*. My mother's sister had been gravely ill for several months, her survival dependent on surgery which was scheduled for the morning of my sailing. One of my brothers, then a surgical resident, assisted at the operation and came home to tell us that the surgery was a complete success and that Nan was going to be fine.

With that good news we all went to the ship in a mind to celebrate. Champagne bottles were opened in the little cabin I was sharing with three other young men. Then several friends from college, more champagne in hand, arrived unexpectedly and as a surprise, so the sailing party was large and great fun. By sailing time my head was spinning from all the champagne, and I had a hard time picking out the familiar faces now milling in the crowd on the dock.

I could see people in the crowd below look up the black hull of that great ship to the railings far above, run their eyes along the railings for the known face, then point and wave. The gangways were retracted, the ropes cast off, and an ordinary traffic light mounted on the river end of the pier changed from red to green. Then, like an obedient little taxi, this thousand-foot liner, the greatest ship in the world, slipped out into the Hudson River.

I was traveling with a shipful of students on their way to graduate studies in European universities. Many had received grants and probably represented the best efforts of our American universities. In those leisurely days of ocean travel we passed our days lying on deck chairs, reading and resting, and continuing the conversations that had been ongoing since the beginning of our studies.

The arrival in Cherbourg, the days in Paris, where I drank in the sights I had so long wanted to see, and then the drive south through the French countryside to Provence all formed the most extraordinary, unbroken adventure. The images, the sounds, and especially the deep, dusty smells of the St. Germain quarter where, like all good American students, I was staying were so many and so varied that I did not have the occasion to think of what I had left behind. Even in those quiet postwar days, when traffic in Paris was so much lighter, and the restaurants always had empty tables, and the buses room for one more person in their open "back porches," the adventure just in being there was all engaging.

The euphoria of those days was very real. But it was also transitory. When it melted away the loss that was part of my conversion surfaced in a painful way. By the new way of life that I was beginning I was, in effect, anticipating the vowed life I would begin to live a few years later. In retrospect I believe that I was grieving for the loss of those important parts of my life which I had fully expected would be mine, but which are not parts of a life lived with vows of poverty, chastity, and obedience.

The loss of the familiar is painful. When the euphoria of conversion dissipates the sense of loss will surface. I think that the convert should be prepared to recognize this loss and grant it a hearing. It is too important a part of what he or she is going through to be dismissed either as the inevitable second thoughts or as temporary cold feet.

I mention this because it is not unusual for people to equate a conversion with the feelings of euphoria they experience at its initial phase. After all, these feelings are what they have experienced up to that point in their conversion. They are involving and can even be quite pleasant if a bit overwhelming.

But with time this can change. They see what they have left behind and the sense of loss causes them to wonder: have I done the right thing; was this turning in my life reasonable, or am I losing my grip; have I tricked myself in putting behind me the life I had?

Here again, it is good to recall that what makes our conversion religious is the goal of the conversion, what we are converted to, not what we are going through. What makes the conversion religious is the goal, not the process. And yet what we experience is just the opposite, the process, not the goal.

So we are faced with a need to go beyond the process to a greater understanding of the goal. As we do so we face a real need to sort out the events current in our lives. In the process of our conversion we may have left behind many good things. But does the goal of our conversion require that they be left behind?

I think of a young man* who came from a family whose members were conscious of their family history and accomplishments, which were notable. During the years of his growing up he had come to associate family life with stoking the fires of family heritage, fitting into a long tradition of family expectations, and supporting the family's concern with its continuity. He experienced a conversion, turned from his family, and joined a religious order dedicated to working with the

* In this example, as in all examples used through this book, sufficient changes are made to disguise the identity of the persons involved and thus protect their privacy.

poor, with people who had no roots, no heritage, and barely any plans for the next day other than the meanest form of survival.

After his conversion, and after some time with his new brethren, he began to think of his family. As he began to see the poor with whom he was sharing his life no longer as a faceless group—"the poor"—but as real people, single individuals, each with his or her own story, he also started to think of his family in the same way. But was it right to do so? Had he not left them behind as part of his conversion, and was it right to turn back from the absoluteness of his new life?

I explained that he had left them behind during the process of his conversion, but that this alienation need not be part of the goal. Christian charity and Christian tradition, after all, speak of the basics of human kindness to which one's own family ought not be strangers.

So he went to visit them, to reestablish ties with them. Here, too, he came to see them not as "family," personless roles against whose life and authority he had reacted, but as concrete individuals. Like him they were each trying to make sense of life using the resources at hand, and not always doing much of a job of it. But he was able to look at their attempt in a more compassionate way and as the difficult human struggle it was.

Granting that the euphoria of conversion will eventually fade away, how can we make sense of the loss, or whatever it is that surfaces, when the expectations of euphoria diminish? I approach this question with my own rational prejudices, but I find no acceptable alternatives to them. So I believe that we should apply reasonable principles. We avoid slogans. We listen to people with sound judgment and good sense. Most of all we avoid religious zealots. And we do so because they commonly equate the first stage of conversion with the entire process.

Zealots also confuse the process of conversion with the goal. The movement toward God as the goal of a conversion is lost sight of in the emotional overflow and enthusiasm of the conversion process. Zealots draw on the imagery in scripture to support their equating of the first stage of conversion with the entire process. They mention that once having put your hand to the plow you must not turn back. You must put off the old man and put on the new. But underlying these statements is their presumption, which has no justification, that the beginning of a conversion with its noise and self-assurance is the same as putting on the new man and holding firm to the plow.

Relating these ideas to my young friend, whom I mentioned above, it was quite appropriate for him to reestablish his family ties. Once the euphoria of his conversion had passed he felt a need to make sense of what he was going through. The separation from his family was experienced as a loss, and he developed a longing to see them. He concluded that for his own integrity he had to fit them, his personal history, and his origins into his new life.

Another aspect of conversion can be a sense of disorientation that comes with losing our hold on the familiar. Conversion can be an upending experience. We can feel at loose ends, even drifting dangerously far from what is safe and familiar.

When I changed my plans to attend law school and decided instead to live in the Dominican priory in Provence I was faced with the need to tell my parents about this major change in my life. "What am I going to say? How do you explain something so strange? They're going to think that I'm losing my grip on reality." And from time to time when the euphoria of my conversion was not so firmly in the saddle I, too, wondered if this might be true.

Our sense of self, or our identity, is often tied up with the people and setting that have been part of the road we have followed in life. When we leave that road for a new one, and leave behind the people and surroundings that were part of it, we also leave behind some of that sense of self. Our identity can become less firm.

A change in our sense of self, our identity, can affect us in different ways. A change in the sense of self at a time of conversion is often experienced as liberating. If the sense of self incorporates burdensome strictures or values, then leaving that sense of self behind will feel liberating. If our sense of self was colored by feelings of unworthiness or guilt for past actions, or was defined by association with people whose attitude toward us was negative or destructive, then leaving those attitudes and those people can feel freeing. If our sense of self was of someone who did not fit in, who was condemned by life to be a spiritually homeless wanderer, then a conversion to a faith and values that provide direction and, perhaps, even a community will be experienced as a welcome relief.

Loosening the reins on our identity, what the psychologists call the ego, can also be a tricky business because it is the ego that is our bridge with reality. A diffuse ego can also be one which is losing contact with what is real, so maintaining some real solidity to the sense of self is important.

The person who is going through a conversion may begin to think at some point that things are going just too fast. Changes may be coming more rapidly than he or she can handle. I would trust that feeling. Our built-in warning systems are there for a purpose. When it seems that the pace of change should slow up, then it should slow up. The purpose of a conversion is to find a new purpose and direction in life, not to melt away the person as a means of getting rid of the old way. The new purpose, we hope, will give the convert more than he or she had in the past by way of a direction in life. But conversion presupposes that there is an ongoing ego, a person, who is being converted. Preserving the basic structures of that self is not a fault, not a surrender to human frailty. It is a simple act of survival.

It is difficult for me to talk about the feelings of conversion without talking about what some people refer to as psychic energy. I don't know whether or not anyone has adequately defined what this means. And I admit I use the phrase feeling as unscientific as a medieval doctor's talk of vapors and humors. But I don't know a better phrase. I can, I think, give examples to explain how this psychic energy, whatever it is, affects us.

To begin with, not knowing what you are going to do with your life and going through motions that you suspect are leading nowhere can be very draining. People who come to the realization that things can't keep going the way they are going and that something just has to give, but who don't know what to do nor where to go, report that living this way is very fatiguing. I suspect that what is being drained away is what is referred to as psychic energy.

On the other hand, people who finally resolve these crises, who decide what they are going to do about the choices facing them, who pull the loose ends of their lives together and arrive at personally satisfying decisions, often react with a sense of relief. Their drive and energy returns, or perhaps appears for the first time. What returns or becomes apparent is psychic energy.

Sometimes the conversion process releases such an amount of psychic energy that it threatens to overwhelm the individual. Whatever the contradictory forces being held together prior to the conversion, albeit in a draining equilibrium, the resolution of the contradiction releases so much energy that for some people it can feel as though the floodgates are being opened.

Here, too, the individual may feel a need to establish order and control in the face of a drive that threatens to become overpowering. This need for restraint does not necessarily bespeak a retreat from the new life. It is only a pulling back from an emotional abundance that is proving more than the individual can handle. Here, too, it is eminently reasonable to decide how much change we can handle. It is not easy for me to believe that reasonable decisions can ever be inappropriate.

3

Conversion as
a Healing Process

From the Siskiyous along the Oregon border to the Tehachapis in the south runs California's great central valley. Bounded on the west by the green and fog-cooled Pacific Coast Range and on the east by the mile-high granite wall of the Sierra Nevada, it is the most generous garden in the world. It is a land of incredibly rich soil and multiple harvests.

For over a hundred years emigrants from less giving lands have come here to set down roots in the rich earth. They established small towns of grange halls and Main Streets, and planted stands of elm and cotton-wood around the simple houses they built to shade them from the power of the summer sun. Many arrived poor, often after a painful journey, bringing little with them other than their courage and their wounds.

Some of them were religious. And of those who were, some gave form to their faith in religions that mirror both the pain of their past and their tenacious optimism for the future. In this land, where all can be made to grow well and straight, they developed religions of healing through faith.

Driving back to Berkeley from a solitary hiking trip into the Sierras I stopped to rest and stretch in one of these little towns. Unshaven, sunburned, and showing the grime of several nights spent sleeping on the ground, I decided I was a little too disreputable-looking for the orderly center of the little town. I parked a few blocks away, next to an unused farm machinery auction lot. Two hours of twisting mountain roads followed by the monotonous drive halfway across the valley had stiffened my arms and back, so I was more aware of my discomfort than of the surroundings as I stepped down from my pickup truck. But as I stretched out my stiff arms and looked around I realized that I was on the edge of uncommon activity.

On the vacant lot a faith healer was supervising a dozen men as they worked to raise her meeting tent. Posters a teenager was stapling to the nearby telephone poles announced that the Healing Power of the Lord God was going to be sent upon Those In Need. And this was to come about, they announced, by the Prayers and the Healing Hands of Sister Eleanor. My tendency to dismiss this without second thought as another kooky California religious event was held in check by the realization that that was Sister Eleanor herself, just thirty feet away from me.

She was a frail-looking, middle-aged woman with what struck me then as an intense and driven quality. Maybe she was just tired. Unlike the excited faithful, she had evidently been through this tent-raising many times before. She took pains to keep their enthusiasm from taking its toll on her equipment, asking them to be careful with the frayed ropes and thinning canvas. The tent went up, as traveled and worn as the faith healer herself.

A sturdy-looking farm wife parked in front of me and brought out a picnic basket filled with enough good food to take care of them both for several days. She invited "S'ter Ellner" to take time from her work and have some lunch. The tired and harassed healer, more accustomed to giving than to receiving, looked hesitantly at the farm woman and the basket. Then she softened very visibly, thanked the woman with genuine appreciation, and sat down with her to eat.

I think of healing, and this image from the past comes to mind. I want to talk about healing because it is a fundamental part of the process of conversion. The conversion that is our principal concern is an entry into the Christian life, and this life is supposed to be a life of healing. But what do we mean by healing in the Catholic tradition? Is it the same as the healing of the faith healer? What is being healed, and how is this accomplished? These are the questions I want to answer in this chapter.

In the church we define healing within a broad context. I want to present the context rather than simply define healing because healing is so important a part of the Christian life, and I do not think it can be understood outside its context. It is complex because it is as broad as our own human situation. Two examples may illustrate.

One morning a strong young man came quickly up the stairs to my office. He had been announced by the receptionist at the church tribunal where I was working, and almost immediately I could hear his athletic step echoing lightly in the stairwell. He walked into my office without waiting for my invitation, and had he asked for my vote in a congressional election it wouldn't have seemed out of place. He was handsome, young, well dressed, and apparently on top of things.

Our meeting that morning, however, had little to do with his abilities and successes, which would have been substantial even for a man at the end of his working career. He and his wife of five years had separated and divorced, and now he was in the process of trying to make sense of that experience. And it had been devastating. He did not speak of their separation or divorce but of "the failure of my marriage." That sense of failure was right under the surface, and whenever he began to think of the divorce his confidence drained from him. As our conversation progressed he slumped farther down into his chair, his voice fell, and he finally ended up just sitting there, looking down, the tears falling freely down his cheeks. He was the picture of a badly shaken man, with his self-esteem undermined and his hope for any permanence in love destroyed.

I think of another situation a thousand miles away. During my years as pastor I worked with members of my parish among desperately poor people along the Mexico-California border. One of these poor was a man, crippled by a work accident, who supported himself and his family by selling fruit to students at the local university. Very early each morning, with pain and difficulty, he would manage to pedal his bicycle to the distant fruit market, purchase what he could afford and could carry, then pedal to the university, where he would spend the day. At dark he then pedaled back to his tiny house.

He followed this unchanging routine every day of the year, year in and year out. His greatest fear was that his strength would fail or he might fall ill. If he were to miss a day, he feared, then someone more aggressive and stronger than he would come and take his place at the university. That place was understood to be his only for as long as he occupied it. He hoped and prayed that his health would allow him to pedal to the fruit sellers at dawn each day, to the university afterward, to return home each night without collapsing in the face of the summer's intense heat, the cold rain of winter, and the inherent weakness in his crippled body.

The pain and the scars in the lives of these two men are readily evident. And their need for healing, different though it may be, is also quite real. The Christian tradition, furthermore, looks at people like this and situations like these not as peripheral to the Christian life but as prime examples of what Christianity is all about. Why is this so? To understand we have to step temporarily into another consideration, an explanation of two key issues. We have to explain what is meant by sin, and we have to explain why sin is viewed principally as a condition, not an action.

It is the teaching of the church that we begin our lives wounded, with a wound that touches the very core of our being. It is this wound that sets us warring within our own selves, one part against the other. It is this same wound, when actualized in our decisions, that leads to our own wrong actions. It is what theologians refer to as original sin.

Speaking of sin commonly involves us in images that do not quite fit the reality. We speak of washing away sin, an image that equates sin with dirt. We speak of forgiving sin, which equates sin with financial indebtedness. We speak of committing sins, which equates sin with our actions. When most of us think of sin, I suspect, we think of actions. We think of people doing things, things they shouldn't be doing. Think for a moment of a preacher discussing sin, and you may well imagine someone telling his people not to do certain things. If we imagine a situation in which sin is being discussed, once again, we probably think of morally bad actions. But the point is that we think of actions.

Now, that is not the principal way sin is viewed in the theological tradition. There, sin is explained first and foremost not as an action but as a condition. It is thought of as the condition of being ill or wounded.

There is a real difference in these two points of view. Why? Because there is a fundamental difference between looking at sins as actions to be condemned and in looking at sin as a wound to be healed. It is the difference between a judge and a healer. The one condemns what is wrong. The other tries to heal what is hurt. In the best of the Catholic tradition the notions of sin as a wound and of life as a process of being healed are the starting points for any consideration of sin.

St. Thomas Aquinas, one of the greatest theologians in the history of the church, addressed this issue directly. Discussing the Christian belief that God became man in the person of Jesus of Nazareth, he first restates the Christian belief that this took place for the forgiveness of sin. Then he asks a question that probably sounds very strange to our twentieth-century ears. He asks whether the entry of God into our world was principally for the forgiveness of our sins, in the plural, or original sin, sin in the singular—the "sin of the world," as it is called in the gospel and in the liturgy. He answers that it is for the forgiveness of original sin. And the rationale he gives in support of the words of the scripture is that original sin is the more serious wound, the source of our own sins, and thus the most in need of healing.

For this reason the theological tradition speaks of sin in the singular. It looks not so much at our bad actions but at our condition, which is likened to an illness. It is common to all, and it is a wound in our nature, a wound that leads us to strive destructively within ourselves and, in the outer world, against one another.

How does this wound, which is such a part of us from the beginning of our lives that we are not personally responsible for it, lead to morally bad actions, the sins in the plural, for which we are responsible? I can answer this question best, I think, by giving examples of this wounded condition in us as it actually affects what we do.

When I became pastor I was asked by the parish council to establish a youth ministry. We had a sizable number of youngsters in our community, and everyone seemed to agree that we needed a means to involve them in the parish. I decided that a program modeled on the Peace Corps would be involving, could mobilize their strengths and idealism, and might also serve as a stimulus to some critical social thinking. I knew that a number of children's shelters in Baja California were in need of help so I decided to make contact with one.

Like many Californians I have traveled in Baja California and have experienced the sense of awe, unchanged with each passage, that comes in crossing the frontier. The prosperity and leisure life of San Diego stand in such stark contrast with the raw poverty so apparent in Tijuana. I have sat in heavy silence as our car sped by the misty arroyos on the south side of the bay and looked on the collection of crate-wood and packing-case hovels on the steep slopes. It was, and continues to be, a relief to reach the sunny oceanside cliffs, with their whitewashed vacation homes set off by potted hibiscus and bougainvillea after this overexposure to reality.

When I began looking for a children's home in need of help my only hope was that it would turn out to be somewhere else, not among the poor in these grim arroyos. Poverty of that kind and depth I wanted to keep not only at a distance but out of sight. I was afraid that I could not handle it.

The fear of not being able to cope with a common human situation, the lot of the poor, is an effect of this wound that we refer to as original sin. This fear becomes a source of our own actual sins—sins in the plural—because it leads us to distance ourselves from these good people simply because of their poverty. It leads us to do wrong because it frightens us into accepting divisions among us, divisions that should not be there. It leads us to do wrong by having us turn our backs on their needs, not because we begrudge them a decent life or wish them ill, but because we are afraid of being overwhelmed by this terrible poverty which is their lot.

On another occasion I was driving in a somewhat similar situation, delivering clothing to families our parish was supporting. It was raining and cold. As we approached the part of the city that was our goal we turned onto a series of unpaved, muddy streets lined on both sides by miserable, soggy shacks barely high enough to stand in. They were made of cardboard, the wood from packing cases, and plastic garbage bags salvaged from the dump. The weight of the rain had bellied down the roofs and canted the walls. Inside, visible through the open door-ways, impoverished families huddled together. As I maneuvered my truck slowly down the slippery street, trying to avoid getting stuck in the velvety mud, one woman with a baby in her arms, misery and cold written on her face, looked right at me. That look was more than I could stand. I tried to think of other things and turned my attention to the road.

Because of my fears these people—just like me except for their poverty—became frightening. These fears, the fear of the poverty in the shacks of the arroyos, and the fear of the desperate people huddled in the rain, these fears are the sin of the world, original sin, as it is written in my own being.

Our own single, individual sins, our personal acts of wrongdoing, are concrete realizations of this wound in our nature. They are the wounded condition carried into action. They, too, are in need of healing. But, to carry the medical analogy further, they are more like symptoms. Their healing occurs with healing the wound that is their source.

How does this healing take place? Within the Catholic tradition, I believe, we see this healing in a broad and a social context. This means a different context than that, for example, of faith healers like Sister Eleanor. We would see sin and healing not only as affecting the individual but as involving society. I will illustrate this by using the example of the crippled fruit seller I mentioned above. Of his several needs for healing the greatest need would actually not be his own, but that of the community that allows him to live so pitifully on its margin. Then, next in the order of priorities, comes his desperate and fearful view of life, a view that may be justified considering his circumstances. But these circumstances and his reaction to them should be replaced by a more hopeful view of life, along with a cause for more hope. Finally, there is the need to heal his crippled body.

I mention these priorities because the priorities of the faith healer would probably be just the opposite. Reflecting the personalist origins of American churches, a subject we will discuss in detail later on, they would be principally individual and personal, and minimally social. This social quality of the Catholic tradition is not a minor or secondary emphasis. It is basic and central and can even be seen as a theological concept touching on the church's very sense of self.

In the gospels Jesus spoke of our condition using a medical analogy. He referred to himself as a doctor come to cure the ill. The gospel narratives describe him curing people, and he used this medical analogy to describe spiritual illnesses. Christians have used this same analogy ever since, and this is why we use it also.

I admit that I find it difficult to encounter faith healing without feeling skeptical in the extreme. I distrust it because it seems magical and superstitious. But I am also prepared to admit the power of the sacraments of the church, sacraments whose power is located in people no less human than faith healers like Sister Eleanor. Perhaps the difference is that the sacraments, in Catholic practice, are so undramatic and minimally concerned with displays of power. Faith healing, to the contrary, seems as much ordered to show the power of the faith healer as it is to heal the sick.

I also recognize that this seemingly superstitious ritual is being carried out by people as genuine and sincere as Sister Eleanor and as kind as the farm wife. The use of prayer to bring healing strikes me as at best an illusion and at worst a hoax. Yet I admit that this is the subjective response of a rational man, as founded on the prejudices of my own logical temperament as on any religious tradition.

This caution about my own motives notwithstanding, I still believe that there is another major problem to be found in the approach of the faith healer. I believe that we can see the faith healer making overconcrete and narrow what is actually broad and symbolic. There is, in the view of the faith healer, a literalism and a narrow focus that distorts the broad view of healing that is part of the Christian tradition. In the Christian view what is to be healed is all of life, not just the ills of the moment. And this view of life is also transcendent, with eternity the ultimate measure.

I believe that the broader view of healing that is part of the Catholic tradition can be symbolized in the church's sacramental life. Baptism is an example of what I mean. It is the practice to baptize infants, and it is the belief of the church that this baptism is for the forgiveness of original sin. In this baptism adult sponsors speak in the name of the child. If we define original sin in light of our plural, personal wrong actions, then this baptism makes little sense. Children, obviously, are not capable of having done anything wrong, and there is no personal wrongdoing to forgive. If we think of the adult sponsors as somehow recanting personal sins in the name of the child, then the error is compounded.

However, if we accept a different definition of sin, if we begin with the notion of sin as a wound and see single bad actions as proceeding from this wound as from a source; if we see this baptism as the beginning of a lifelong process of being healed, and the presence of the sponsoring adults as their statement that they will support this child as the wounds common to all humankind are healed, then the baptism does make sense. To be afraid of the challenges of life while growing up, to seek isolation when feelings are hurt, and to want to retaliate when injured, the child does not have to be evil. All he has to be is a human, a human in need of healing. For to be human means to start out in life wounded. Christian life is a lifelong process of healing this wound.

The process of initiation into the life of the church should itself be a process of healing, and it should be an entry into a life of healing. This is why the rites of initiation speak of healing. The medical analogy is appropriate for the entire Christian life because it was used by Christ to describe his own work.

The role that healing plays in the Christian life, furthermore, is fundamentally different from its role in religious cults. Religious cults founded on healing, some of which are at least nominally Christian, see healing as an event that takes place at the moment of conversion and as a prelude to the living of the converted life. The cult community is the gathering of the healed, and the life of the cult community is a celebration of the fact that they have been healed. In Christianity, on the other hand, while there is a recognition that healing has begun and a firm hope that it will be accomplished, the life of the Christian is very much one of a person always on the way. Healing is not the prelude to Christian living. It is its substance.

For me it is comforting to see healing as a necessary part of our entire life. It means that we do not have to pretend that we have been healed when we know, in fact, that we still have far to go. We can be thankful for the healing that has already taken place in our lives, while still recognizing that our need for further healing remains very real.

At the beginning of this chapter I drew on my recollection, many years old, of Sister Eleanor. She was brought out of her burdened state by the kindness of a generous farm woman. In a sense, the healer was healed through the ordinary human commerce of a picnic lunch together. In the Catholic tradition we see this continuing process of people sharing their lives as a chief means of the healing we receive. It lies at the heart of our sacraments, which are ordinary human relationships given a sacral and saving quality. It underlies our community life and is also one of its chief purposes. It is in this light that we can see the convert looking to the Christian life and the Christian community for healing.

II

Election

"In the beginning I couldn't square my scientific training and scientist's approach with faith. My life is spent in finding proof for things. So I find it very helpful to know how other people resolve questions of faith and knowledge. Some people, it seems, get inspirations. Others, like me, have to work things through on a very human level. The year-long catechumenate experience gave me the context for this working-through."

FROM MARGARET'S ACCOUNT OF
HER CONVERSION

MARGARET'S STORY

An Account of My Election to the Catholic Church

By temperament some people are religious. Faith and believing come naturally to them. I am not one of these natural believers. Faith, for me, comes only with difficulty. It has been a problem and it remains a problem.

I grew up in a Protestant family in Omaha. My first recollections of religion, which cover the years up to the time that I was twelve, are of being sent off to Sunday school while my parents remained in bed. In our church children really took no part. We were sent off to Sunday school, which was incredibly boring, and we were never allowed to be present for worship, except on rare occasions like Christmas and Easter. As a result I grew up finding little purpose in going to church.

Then, when I was twelve, my family moved to a different part of town. Our house was close to an Episcopal church which my mother and I began attending. Since I had been baptized as a child I simply had to begin attending. I found this parish, especially its liturgy, more fulfilling, and I attended until I went away to college.

In my last year in high school I had begun to realize that I had real questions. These questions grew, aided by the fact that many of my friends were not believers. They were raising existential questions, such as "Does God exist or not?" And they all answered "How can we know?" and nobody had any answers. By this time I had stopped participating, attending only with my parents at Christmas and Easter.

And then, after college, I moved out here to Berkeley. I met my husband, who had been raised a Catholic. But like many Catholics who no longer believe, he had become a fairly convinced anti-Catholic and antireligious man. He couldn't see why anybody would want to have anything to do with any kind of religion. Many of his friends, and the other people I met here, had the same ideas. Religious questions were not vital issues here, but there was always the underlying belief that, in any event, religion made no sense at all.

Our friends here were politically involved in liberal and radical movements. This was in the middle to late sixties and the climate in Berkeley was very political. We were married in an Episcopal church, but that was purely to please my parents. When my first child was born I thought of baptism just as a matter of course, but my husband said no because that involved religious promises which he was not prepared to observe. With our second child the issue never even came up.

However, for a number of years I had had some religious questions, probably the same ones that got asked and never answered when I was in college. I had talked about religion with friends, but none of the questions ever became serious. And the questions continued to rumble around within me.

My children raised religious questions which I couldn't answer, and our babysitter, a very devout, Bible-reading evangelical, often provided religious answers to every question. But I really didn't want to talk about religion seriously.

What eventually brought the religious issue out into the open was a thoroughly nonreligious matter, our children's education. We decided that they needed a better education than they were getting in the public schools and knew that the local Catholic schools were a good alternative. My husband's anti-Catholic attitudes had been softening, so he was willing to consider this. And the fact that he is a baptized Catholic, his own lack of belief notwithstanding, makes him officially a Catholic. So, for purely pragmatic reasons, we went and registered at the local Catholic parish. It was purely and simply an educational strategy. Like many people in Berkeley we were prepared to do anything to escape the turmoil in the school system.

At that point I decided that if my children were to be in Catholic schools I should begin to attend Mass just to find out what was going on. I also decided to send them to Sunday school as my parents had sent me. The school director understood my thinking perfectly and turned me down cold. I could bring the kids to Sunday school only after our family, as a family, attended Mass for a year or so.

My husband actually agreed to go for a while, but he prepared me for the worst. No one talks to anyone else, he said. People are both insulated and isolated. It is cold, unfriendly, and silent.

Our first Sunday turned out to be Palm Sunday. The very first thing the congregation did was leave the church, walk around the block in a Palm Sunday procession while singing hymns, and then, after Mass, gather in the parish social center for a very friendly reception. This was not what we were expecting at all.

In addition, the liturgy proved to be a very moving experience for me. I had the feeling that this is what I had been looking for. The community was open. And I began to suspect that I was more ready to deal with religious issues than I had thought.

When I decided to enroll the children in the parish school I went and met with one of the priests, who told me that they were beginning a series of classes for people interested in knowing more about the beliefs of the church. At that point my interest was more for the sake of supporting the kids' education. It was not a personal one. The program turned out to be a combination of instructions and personal stories. I did not find the lectures particularly enlightening, but once the participants began to share their own human stories of religious searching I found that my own interest came alive.

During this time it was suggested to the people in the group that we all get sponsors, as required for the rites of initiation. Most of the people there had already decided to become Catholics, and that was why they were there. I was there for other reasons, but when the question of a sponsor came up I decided to ask for one. That, it seems, was the concretization of my decision to become a Catholic. How conscious was this decision? I don't know. In retrospect it certainly seems to lack the clarity of purpose and mind in which I take such pride. At the least my decision was more gradual than it was with the others. In any event the change from where I was when I first started asking religious questions to the place I was at at the time of my election was considerable.

My husband was, and remains, taken aback by my reaction. He finds it hard to understand how anyone can believe. He likes the community, he enjoys the singing, he is supportive of me, and he attends Mass with us. But his problems with faith and his lack of belief remain the same.

I admit that I have not resolved all the matters of faith myself. Essentially, I did not join a belief, I joined a community. I wanted to be a part of this community and what they had. I knew that I could continue to attend Mass without becoming a Catholic, but that was not the same. I wanted to be a part of this people. So I simply put questions of faith aside, and I am working them out as I go along.

The length of the catechumenate, and for me it was a year, was very helpful. I needed that year. Especially I needed to see how these issues were worked out in other people's lives. In the beginning I couldn't square my scientific training and scientist's approach with faith. My life is spent in finding proof for things. So I find it very helpful to know how other people resolve questions of faith and knowledge. Some people, it seems, get inspirations. Others, like me, have to work things through on a very human level. The year-long catechumenate experience gave me the context for this working-through.

One of my friends described what I am doing as a suspension of disbelief. I think that this description is accurate. What is happening with me, over a period of time, is that the two parts, the scientific and the religious, are just slowly coming together. But I have to admit that, unlike some people, I am not all that troubled by their separation. In fact, because of my scientific work I actually find it more helpful to keep them separate. I am not going to look for proof in my faith. And I certainly don't want to lose my critical sense in my work. But the two do come together in some organic way over the course of time, and I find that I can cope with my suspension of disbelief.

For example, there is no proof that the Holy Spirit is working in my life. And yet that seems to be happening. I can see this in my life not because of proofs or explanations but because others describe it in their own lives, and I can see the parallels in my life. I was discussing this with one of the catechumens, telling him that I thought I had probably wanted to come into the church for quite a while but was afraid to face all the personal and family issues I would have to face. And then, circumstances just seemed to play my cards for me. "Well," he said as a very simple statement, "that was probably just God tugging at you." I would never think that way. But having someone else say it helped me to bridge between what I saw as my world of reason and their world of religion.

For me, perhaps because I have this scientist's approach to life, I find that the kind of very pious religion that others have could never be mine. My faith does not involve having God run the ordinary details of my day. Once, when our group of catechumens was talking about God's role in our lives, someone began to describe how she prays to God for almost everything—from finding parking places to making the dishwasher work. I was quite impressed with this faith, and was prepared to admit that it was the only real faith. I also knew that it could never be mine and wondered where that left me.

But after discussions with one of the priests in our parish I came to realize that this was more a matter of temperament. Some people tend to relate everything to ultimate causes. I, on the other hand, who not only work as a scientist but think as one, am always looking for the most proximate causes. The religious approach of these two persons is going to be different. I have come to see that this difference is not good or bad, just different. And there is room for each of us in the church.

The rite of election was a very moving experience. It took place during Lent at the cathedral. We say, speaking symbolically, that God calls each person by name. As the central act in this rite of election each one of the three hundred fifty of us was called by name. And for me the symbol came alive. The act of being called and chosen really sank in.

This rite was the first that really seemed to be a milestone. Our sponsors went with us to the cathedral and at that time, as during the whole preparation period, I found myself becoming very emotional. My friends among the catechumens and my sponsors understood my reaction. This was affirming at a time when I needed affirmation, and it felt very supportive.

During this time of election and preparation I found it difficult to combine the different parts of my life. I was so involved in the religious conversion I was going through that the ordinary tasks of life were not getting done. Taxes, for example, come up at this time of year, and in the April of my election and preparation for entering the church they just didn't get done. My friends began to wonder about me. And I myself even began to wonder if I might be going a little crazy. I could not go to church without ending up in tears. The ordinary routines of life, which I usually find enjoyable, began to seem pale. My emotions were very close to the surface.

This personal reaction came to a head in my need to deal with the sacrament of penance. Going to confession was one of those few things that I really dreaded. Not that there was anything particularly secret or evil I had to reveal. Rather it was a matter of putting behind me some things which my rational side knew were not sins but which were in the way. I was too involved with our parish priests to want to talk with them. Not knowing what to do about confession, I asked a Catholic friend, who told me to make an appointment at the adjacent university parish, which I did. Our discussion was surprisingly, and helpfully, low-keyed. The priest with whom I talked told me, of course, that these matters were not sins. But he prayed for me, in what he called a healing of memories. It was very helpful. Not only was I able to move ahead, feeling that these irrational but real roadblocks had been removed, I also felt for the first time that I belonged.

The rite of election was for me more a conclusion than a beginning. The whole process of conversion I had been going through brought issues to the surface that had been stewing in me, it seems, for a long time. There were childhood memories of going to church, the questions and doubts of my college years, all the social activism and antireligious liberalism of the 1960s, and the lack of a religious sense in our family. These were not the issues that were raised initially: we went to Mass as a strategy to help our kids' education. But once we were attending church I found that these issues came to the surface in a way I hadn't anticipated. And though they surfaced with apparent ease, once they were out in the open I began to realize how strongly I felt about them.

It was at this time that I began to appreciate the faith sharings we had in our group of catechumens. We had all kinds of people—people from Protestant backgrounds, from Jewish backgrounds, from no religion. And hearing them share their stories, describing very different kinds of personal histories, and articulate their religious views and needs made me aware how different people really are. It was not just that I was different. Everyone was different. That difference helped me to see that I could come into the church not having to fit in, but as the person I am, with all my own ways.

The rite of election, which took place at the cathedral, further helped me appreciate these differences. But at the cathedral these differences took on the note of universality. There were hundreds of catechumens there, different races, all different backgrounds, and from this you could see the worldwide nature of the church.

The universality, the worldwide community, is important to me. Even the public dimension draws me. One of the things that I need at this point is to go beyond my own little world. Perhaps it is the Berkeley background with its emphasis on the role of society. And in this I think we have come full circle, for once again we are talking about basic social issues. But this social action is no longer carried on by people fleeing their faith. It is founded on religious values.

I see the church as today's effective society. It is made so effective because it combines real faith and ritual. The faith is personal, but the participation is sufficiently ritualized that it allows all of us to take part without having to overpersonalize. If I had to stand up and proclaim, in a very personal way, why I wanted to become a Catholic I would never have done it. But being involved, with others, in a public, group election was very helpful. There was a sense that my move into the church was irrevocable, like getting married. My immersion into the life of the church and its liturgy, which was symbolized so forcefully at the time of the rite of election, has given me the sense that the church is really a basic part of me.

4

The Role of the Community

Conversion begins within the spirit of the individual. It begins as an individual and personal experience. But for conversion to become an integral part of the person it must be expanded to include the people and circumstances that make up the individual's life. Otherwise, it runs the risk of becoming some secret or idiosyncratic interest, outside the mainstream of life.

The second stage of the initiation into the church is called the rite of election. This rite recognizes the need to channel the elements in an individual's conversion from the inner place of their origins to the outside world. It is well designed to connect the convert's inner life with the people and circumstances that are the convert's world.

Election takes place in a public ceremony. In this ceremony the convert is admitted into the final stage of preparation for full membership in the church. The rite of election is jarringly public. To give the ritual a specially public quality the celebrant is supposed to be the bishop. This suggests that all the converts within the diocese be gathered together for the ceremony, either in the cathedral or some other equally large and public place. The convert and his or her sponsors stand before the gathered community and are questioned by the celebrant, bishop or priest, about the individual's readiness for the new way of life. Given the Western assumption that religion is a personal and private matter, the public quality of the election rite can feel startling.

The rite of election also presupposes that the priest is comfortable with rituals and with the sacral side of his role. This presumption may be unfounded. Priests today are called on to function as community leaders, providers of social services, preachers, and teachers. These roles permit a more personal way of relating than is fostered by the less conscious, almost primitive quality of the priest's functioning in the rite of election. Clergy roles today often involve more familiarity and equality than was common with the ritualized roles of the past.

The primitive quality of the rite is not without its purpose. Among other things it indicates the fundamental level and organic manner in which the individual becomes a part of the community. It also identifies the community with the church. In the first section of this book we looked principally at the situation of the individual in the initial stage of the process of conversion. In this part, following Margaret's account of her election, I want to look at the other end of the initiation relationship, the community into which the convert moves.

During the course of the church's history community has been defined in very different ways. The differences have been significant, even to the point of affecting history. Religious wars have been fought for reasons that strike us as inadequate to justify violence, such as the drive to purify the community or to establish the place of authority in the community. While the different definitions of community we come across today have none of the fanaticism of past centuries, they remain significantly different, and they can affect the community's life. I want to summarize three of the more common views. Then we will describe the view of community that is embodied in the church's rite of election and in its life in general. Finally, we will look at a few common and reoccurring views of community, views that can appeal to the convert because of the dynamics of the conversion process, but which prove to be somewhat bizarre in the actual living.

One of America's leading religious sociologists, Professor Robert Bellah of the University of California, Berkeley, has described the changes in the patterns of America's religious identity. He has made use of a conceptual framework which is commonly used by sociologists. It is also useful to the amateur because it helps us to understand religious life in the United States.*

The framework was developed by Ernst Troeltsch, one of the founders of modern religious sociology. In 1912 he published a study in which he divided Christian institutions into three types: the church type, the sect type, and mysticism. Speaking of these different types Professor Bellah uses the vocabulary of the professional student of religion. He speaks, for example, of the "ontological priority" of the different types in relation one to the other. In less technical terms this refers to the question of which comes first, the community or the individual. Does the community give rise to the believing individual? Or is it the believing individuals who come together to form the community?

Bellah describes the church type as "an organic conception of the religious institution for which the defining metaphor is the Pauline image of the body of Christ." In this view "the church has a certain temporal and even ontological priority over the individual" because "it is in and through the church that the individual believer comes to be what he or she is." This priority of the church over the individual, especially in the order of causes, is a key element in the "church type's" understanding of community.

The sect type of Christian institution, to the contrary, is a voluntary body of believers. Within the sect, as Professor Bellah writes, "the individual believer has a certain priority over the church in that the experience of grace has been seen as temporally prior to admission to membership, even though once admitted, collective discipline can be quite strong."

The sectarian church "sees itself primarily as the gathered elect and focuses on the purity of those within as opposed to the sinfulness of those without." Means to make this distinction between the pure and the sinful take on an importance they do not have in the church type of institution, because life there is seen much more in shades of gray.

The very idea of election may give the impression that the church's rite of election is partly sectarian in its functioning. Because of the importance of sects in American religious life today the rite of election can, in fact, appear to fit into a larger pattern of common, sectarian religious experience. But while the process of election does attempt to

* "Power and Religion in America Today," *Commonweal,* December 3, 1982.

confirm an individual's turning from one kind of life to a new one, as we shall see it is not by leading him or her into a sect.

Troeltsch's third type of religious institution, the mystical type, sounds foreign to our experience. Mysticism is simply not a part of American life. However, what he means by it is very American. He is really talking about religious individualism. And that is about as American as you can get. According to religious sociologists it is the most common form of religious expression in the United States. So it is an important element in our view of conversion.

Troeltsch's categories are useful because they are clear and because they match the kinds of religious experience that are common today. They can help us understand the workings of the church that has been traditional to Catholic Christianity. They can help us understand the appeal and dynamics of evangelical groups. And they can indicate what it is that comes in between a merely cultural Christianity at one end of the spectrum and religious zealotry at the other.

Professor Bellah's studies relate these ideas to common religious experience in America today. Knowing where the typical Americans start out religiously, we can appreciate how they will see the rite of election. We can also understand how they will understand the word community that appears so often in the election process. This is an important consideration, because the way community is understood in the sectarian situation and in more institutionally organic Christianity, like the Catholic Church, is not the same.

What is this "church type" of institution? Rather than simply give a definition I prefer to use several illustrations. Richard Rodriguez talks about his faith and his church in his remarkable autobiography, *Hunger of Memory*. He describes his parents' Mexican Catholic experience.

> The steps of the church defined the eternal square where children played and adults talked after dinner. He remembers the way the church building was at the center of town life. She remembers the way one could hear the bell throughout the day, telling time. And the way the town completely closed down for certain feastdays. He remembers that the church spire was the first thing he'd see walking back into town.

In this experience of church, faith not only defines what you believe but, much more, it defines who you are. There is no distinction between the sphere of religion and the sphere of secular activities, for, as in the town of Rodriguez's father, the church building is at the center of town life. That the priest and the mayor might vie for influence in a situation of this kind, and at times might even be bitter enemies, is not the point. The mayor's traditional anticlericalism is an almost expected offshoot of a church which says not only what you believe but who you are.

"I am the vine. You are the branches." An organic image taken from the gospels. A living being, like a family with a consciousness of its origins, its present, and its future, and like a town with the church at its center and in which all are *católicos*. No distinction is made between those who are and those who are not, since all are. "Anyone who does not remain in me is like a branch that has been thrown away—he withers." Another literally organic image also taken from the gospels. Here, too, there is no talk of other vines and other branches. It is this vine that defines life.

So it was with me and my own sense of being a Catholic, a sense that was bred into me. My parents were Catholic, their families were Catholic, and we, the children, were Catholic. That does not mean that we were religious. None of us was sent to religious schools, nor did we receive anything but the most minimal religious training. I was sent to catechism classes for two months prior to receiving my first communion, which did not happen until I was eleven years old, four years older than was customary. And no priest ever set foot in our house. They had their place, and it was most definitely not in our house.

My father had the same two comments which summed up his view of our parish clergy, and which he would announce to no one in particular as we drove home from Sunday Mass. "The ignorant leading the ignorant," was the first one. After a few blocks came the second. "Preaching is their stock in trade. You'd think they'd learn how to do it."

The disdain my parents felt for the priests in our town, and which their respect for the church kept them from explaining to us, in no way affected the fact that they were Catholics, any more than the fact that Roosevelt was president affected the fact that they were Americans. They went to Mass every Sunday (with us very firmly in tow). They observed Friday abstinence and Lenten fasts. They were solidly Catholic. And they were just as convincedly anticlerical.

What did we believe? Whatever the church believed. How did you know what that was? Principally by reading. We had all been taught the fundamentals of the faith in the Baltimore Catechism. This was a simple question-and-answer presentation of beliefs in which I was drilled by my mother. She focused on the rhythm of the statements and always seemed bemused by the entire process. The first statements had a three-beats-per-measure structure, much like the tunes we played in the kindergarten rhythm band. She seemed to think that if I got the beat down the words would probably follow.

There was more to it than these simple questions and answers, but they were adequate for minds in the making. Once real interests surfaced they could be nurtured by reading histories that detailed the growth and expansion of the church throughout the centuries. In addition there were theological works written by the few intelligent and educated priests. That there were only a few of them did not matter. In my parents' view intelligence and ability were rare commodities in any situation, and the church was no exception. And only a few were needed.

One Easter when I was still quite young I asked my father, who by training was an accountant, the meaning of the word paschal. He used my question to explain the Easter symbolism in some detail. *Pesach*, he said, was the Hebrew word for passover, and he went on to explain the symbolism of the paschal lamb and the Easter liturgy. With the trust of youth I simply assumed that these were the things that everyone's father knew.

But such assumptions were not made about our priests. We discounted most if not all that we heard and saw in the local parish. The priests were uneducated. And many of the people in the parish were Italian and had their own particular kind of piety. The church produced much that was eccentric or troubling, but that was all the product of uneducated clerical minds or Italian piety. Neither of these need be taken seriously. Truth was to be found, but elsewhere.

How did you distinguish between good and bad Catholics? You didn't. Catholics were Catholics. To be a bad Catholic meant, in effect, to be institutionally outside the church. A bad Catholic was someone who was cutting his ties with the church by giving his allegiance to some group that defined itself in opposition to the church, like the Masons or the Protestants. And this was an act of disloyalty. In this view of the church there were few virtues more important and few vices worse than loyalty and disloyalty.

The few people who "lost their faith" were in a different category. Faith was a gift of God, and if someone simply no longer believed that, too, was a reality. It was accepted as a sad and troubling reality, like illness and death. But it was not the same as the Catholic who joined the Masons or became a Presbyterian for business or social purposes. And anyone who did the latter did so, obviously, for those reasons. That you would change your church was an act of disloyalty and, like all the actions of the disloyal, the result of base motives.

In this social and organic view of the church membership comes about naturally, at the time of birth. Not that you are born into the church. Membership is dependent on choice, the choice of the parents for baptism. But that choice is an expected one, similar to the expectation that an adult will register to vote, and will vote when the election day comes. As part of who you are you will baptize your children and raise them as Catholics.

I can recall the adults gathered in our living room asking what to contemporary ears might sound like a vague question, a question about new neighbors or prospective business partners. "What are they?" There was no doubt what that question was asking. "Catholic," came the reply, or Lutheran, or whatever it might be. Occasionally the answer was bleak, as much a commentary on the people as on their religion. "They're not anything." You did not have much to do with people who were not anything.

This same organic view of the church occasioned another comment, which has little meaning outside that context. "He's not a Catholic, but he ought to be." How can faith be a matter of ought? When it is a part of who you are, because identity has its own imperatives.

Another mark of this organic church that I knew was the intentionally static quality of its worship. Our Protestant friends would remark about their own worship that "church was good today" or "it isn't as good with this new minister." How could church be good or bad? Church was church. It was a formal, ritualized, public worship. Its only variations were the structured ones called for by the different seasons. During this ritual people had the opportunity to attend or not to their own private prayers.

The community which precedes the individual is also a mark of this organic church. In this context the convert is a bit of an oddity. In some ways an asset and a valued member, because he or she validates our own identity through the personal choice to take on that identity. And in some ways converts are unsettling, because they raise the image of religious mobility. When religion is a question of identity, religious mobility suggests fluidity in an area that, for personal and social survival, is supposed to be fixed. Consequently, integrating the convert into a church that values stability presents some special challenges. It is probably no accident that, until the renewal of the catechumenate and the rite of election, converts were received into the church in simple, private ceremonies.

This organic and cultural view of religion also creates its own set of problems. There is a form of religion which does not require faith and which is principally cultural. Religious practices of traditionally Christian countries run the risk of falling into this category, of becoming no more than ritual supports to a national sense. This is especially true of countries at moments of national fervor, and in countries looking for religious supports to totalitarian government. The current antireligious trend in Western countries makes this less apparent today, but most of the parties to the world war went into battle with each other blessed and prayed over by their own Christian clergy.

In strong contrast with the "church type" of Christian institution, the organic body I have been describing, is the "sect type." As Professor Bellah points out, the sect focuses on "the purity of those within as opposed to the sinfulness of those without." Unlike the church, where membership ordinarily precedes personal religious awakening for the large majority of members, the sect calls people together only insofar as they have experienced a personal religious choice. As a consequence the sect, unlike the church, attempts to keep the experience of that choice alive as its prime religious function.

Recent American literature has reached some of its high points both in describing this effort and in portraying its effects on the sectarians. Flannery O'Connor's images of the saved struggling to keep free of the sins that come chasing after them are especially noteworthy. One of her typically eccentric creatures, the fourteen-year-old Francis Tarwater, thinks about his dead uncle whose body he is trying to bury. "His uncle had taught him figures, reading, writing, and history beginning with Adam expelled from the Garden and going on down through the presidents to Herbert Hoover and on in speculation toward the Second Coming and the Day of Judgment." It was this same uncle who had rescued the boy from a nonbelieving relative. The Lord himself "had sent him a rage of vision, had told him to flee with the orphan boy to the farthest part of the backwoods and raise him up to justify his Redemption."†

What is metaphor in the literature of O'Connor becomes reality in the lives of some people. There are sectarians, men and women, who struggle to preserve the election they believe given to them to save them from a sinful world.

It is easy to associate the sect type of church with images like those to be found in the works of O'Connor, or in Elmer Gantry, and in the process dismiss it as something fanatical. It would be just as easy to associate the church type with extremes in solidly Catholic countries, such as the pictures of military dictators in Latin countries lined up elbow to elbow with the countries' bishops as, together, they review honor guards on the national holidays. Each of these, the sectarian fanatic and the religious totalitarian, has been and continues to be a part of our world. But they also are caricatures.

Just as the church type, with its organic and culturally based religious life, can become nothing more than a cultural phenomenon, so the sect type, with its concerns for the religious purity of its members, can become nothing more than a study in obsessive behavior. To accept these partial views as total pictures is to sell the religious reality short. I would prefer to consider the sect type of Christian institution at its best, picturing it as it makes a positive and creative contribution to the Roman Catholicism that I know.

This will not be easy because I am not a partisan of this view. Even at its best the sect type of institution strikes me as eventually undermining the theology and life of the church. And it will do so because it presupposes that the experience of grace is, of its nature, prior to and independent of the life of the church. The sectarian community, at heart, seems to me to be the concretization of a psychological process. It is founded on one stage in the process of conversion. It is the conversion process at its most personally convincing and individually liberating. The sectarian religious group is an attempt to turn a psychological

† "You Can't Be Any Poorer Than Dead," *The Complete Stories* (New York: Farrar, Straus and Giroux, 1982), p. 292.

process into an institution. Ironically enough the discipline within sectarian groups often proves to be quite strict.

However, the human experiences that become the sectarian institution are, in themselves, positive and perhaps even necessary in the move of an individual from a religious awakening into a religiously integrated life. For this reason if no other, an attitude that even to me seems narrowly begrudging, the sectarian experience deserves to be presented in a positive light. In any event, the sectarian view of the church is with us, it merits an exposition, and probably a more partisan one than I can give.

I am not hard pressed to find that exposition. I hear it in the churches here in California, and I hear it in our own Dominican chapels. The single, personal experience of faith; the difference between those without and those within; the fervent hope that those without will be brought to the conversion that will bring them in; the working assumption that baptized Catholics who have not had this conversion experience are to be numbered among the outsiders, and that converted non-Catholics have more in common with the elect than their unconverted religious confreres.

The view of the church that is held by members of the sectarian institutions is different from the view held in organic institutions, like the Catholic Church. In the sectarian view the church essentially is the sum of its members. That it might be more than the sum of its members would be a puzzling idea more than it would be a problem.

I want to illustrate the understanding of church as it functions in the lives of Christians who belong to sect-type institutions. Perhaps the most useful example would illustrate the centrality of the conversion experience. I suspect that nothing in their religious lives has the power that is to be found in their moment of conversion. The personal experience of conversion becomes the measure against which all subsequent experiences are judged. In moments of crisis there is a return to this golden moment for strength and for guidance.

I think of a series of discussions with a young man, a student for the priesthood. He was well advanced in his studies of theology and was at the stage where a final decision had to be made about going on for ordination or leaving the seminary. And he found himself in crisis. The crisis, as he presented it, was the conflict between the life to which he felt called and his inability or unwillingness to live a celibate life.

As we discussed his situation it became apparent to me that his interest in the people and work that constitute so much of priestly life was minimal. He said he was bored by church work and disinterested in people and their needs. In fact he seemed not to like people that much. His own recreational projects were his chief interest. His ministerial involvements changed with some regularity, as did his friends. Put together, these qualities pictured for me a young man totally unsuited for the priesthood.

Why in the world was he in a seminary? Because in his college days he had had a conversion experience, and during that experience he felt called to the priesthood. In moments when he saw the incongruity between his predatory sex life and temperament on the one hand and, on the other, the life for which he was studying, he would recall his conversion, his sense of being called, and he would dig in for a few more months.

Interestingly enough, the criteria commonly used in deciding whether or not a young man should continue studying for the priesthood were ignored. Did he like the life? Did he want to help people? Was he interested in working in the church? Was the religious welfare of others important to him? Could he cope with the stresses of a celibate life of service to others? Did he believe what the church believed? Questions that to many would appear no more than common sense were ignored, both by the young man and by his religious mentors.

But these questions come out of the organic life of the church type of community. They were not used to decide whether he was or wasn't suited for the priesthood because he was in a community in which the predominant influence was sectarian. And they were ignored, I suspect, because the community members were all impressed principally by his conversion, his sense of being called, and by their own sense of moral obligation to respond to that personal, individual, religious experience.

This young man, and the counselors who encouraged him to continue in his studies for the priesthood, are examples of the sect view of the church at work. He and they were concerned that the purity of his conversion not be compromised by abandoning a ministry to which he had been called.

In this approach two issues which I see to be important functions of the sectarian view stand out clearly. First, they were all prepared to admit that his conversion constituted him in a specially graced life. That his own personal morality was objectively no better than that of people whom they would see as outsiders, the unconverted and ungraced, was not an issue. The difference between the two was not the moral quality of their lives, but the fact of conversion.

Second, his membership in the church, at least his membership as a living and vital part of the church (he had been baptized a Catholic as a child), was tied to the personal choice he made at the time of his conversion. He had decided to be a Christian and a priest as part and parcel of the same one act and choice that constituted his conversion. To go back on that choice, in all its integrity, would be to go back on his new life.

What brought the young man to me was his inability to cope with the demands of celibacy. Failure in this area at least had the benefit of being somewhat involving and, given traditional attitudes toward the celibacy of the clergy, not easy to dismiss. It also, and finally, provided him with an acceptable reason for going against his "call" and leaving the seminary. Only by connecting his sectarian principles about absolute commitment to the fact that he was vowing to live one way and then living another was I able to give him a usable context for making this decision. My initial suggestions, along the line of the questions I mentioned above, were not helpful to him.

The theology that comes out of the church type differs from the theology of the sect type. Traditional Catholic theology would judge his fitness for the priesthood using human criteria. The questions I listed above would be typical. This kind of theological view would be used not because it is pragmatically helpful, as true as that might be, but because it is human. It is a function of a theology founded on a trust of the human and developed using human nature to flesh out the religious truth. It is a part of human living in an organic way, the same organic way that the branches are an organic and living part of the vine in the parable of Jesus.

The sect type of theology would find these reasons worldly, nonspiritual, and unable to encompass the graced reality of choice and conversion. For the sectarian the conversion experience is the moment of grace. It is this experience which, taken collectively, creates the church.

In the organic view of Christian initiation the moment of conversion would be seen as one religious experience, one among many, in the life of the individual. The drama and importance of the moment would be recognized and in no way undervalued. But it would be no more a sign of God's presence in the life of the individual than the ability to live a good life. In fact, the long-term good life, even an undramatic one, would probably be given the edge in a match to decide where the hand of God could be seen. And the good life of the ordinary Christian would be seen in relation to the individual's incorporation into the church.

Each view, the sect view and the church view, is limited. They are also very different one from the other. The difference is not some fine point to be quibbled over by theologians. It has to do with the role of the human community in bridging the gap between God and the individual. The sect view, taken to the extreme, says there need be no bridge. The church view, also taken to the extreme, says there is no gap. In the sectarian view the relationship between God and the individual needs no mediation. In the organic and cultural view of the church, membership in the church bridges the gap between God and the individual because the church is an extension of Christ in this world.

I want to explain the difference between the two views at greater length. And then, after looking into the third of Troeltsch's types which Professor Bellah mentions, mysticism, I want to provide a synthesis of the three views. As you may suspect, my synthesis will fall more on the side of the "church type" than the "sect type." We can understand the difference between the first two types if we look at the third, or mysticism. As we noted above, this is the equivalent of religious individualism.

Religion in America is a personal and private affair. "My religion is my business." How often have I thought that, and how typically American is that thought. "What I believe is my own private business, and no one has the right to go checking up on my beliefs." We believe this. We have this belief bred into us. And we are surprised to find that other peoples have no appreciation for this point of view.

I recall standing on the old Temple Mount in Jerusalem, the Dome of the Rock a few hundred feet away, and thinking that on this esplanade so many of the events of the gospels took place. Christ himself walked and taught here; the life of the Jewish people was centered here for centuries before; and so much of the history of the world has had this very spot as its focus ever since. An old Arab must have noticed me in my musings. He caught my attention, eye to eye, and with his hand said no. I did not have the right to pray or meditate there. This is Arab territory, it is for Believers. Christians cannot pray here. "You have your own place."

For him, and for an entire people, religion is essentially public. Where you pray is everyone's business, because prayer is not only public but proprietary. If I pray there, then it becomes my land. And he wanted me to know that we had plenty of Christian shrines in Jerusalem, I needn't pray in theirs.

Some weeks later, incidentally, I witnessed members of the Gush Emunim, the "band of the faithful," the Jewish extremist group whose attempts to establish settlements on the West Bank in violation of Israeli law have been well covered by American TV news, attempt to enter onto the Temple Mount for public prayer. They were wearing prayer shawls, they carried a Scroll of the Law of the kind and size used in synagogue worship, and they were dressed for Sabbath service. It was as clear to them as it was to the Arab and Israeli police who stopped them that their actions were as proprietary as religious. They were trying to pray on the Temple Mount as a means to establish legal title to it. Again, prayer in this situation was communal, not individual, and it was essentially public, not private.

We see these actions, or read of similar ones, and are moved to scorn or to wondering "What in the world is wrong with these people?" Religion is personal and private, and it is otherworldly and spiritual if it is anything. That people should be fighting over land in the name of religion, so say we, is not only bizarre and primitive, it is theologically incorrect. To the religious person it is, perhaps, even blasphemous.

So I think. But I think this as an American who is steeped in American religious individualism. As an American I can feel out of place in Catholic shrines in Europe, and except for a few notable exceptions I have felt like an observer and an outsider in the few religious ceremonies I have attended in places Catholic for centuries. The Catholics fervently marching and praying in Lourdes are they, not I.

By contrast I felt quite comfortable walking up San Francisco's Market Street in the early 1960s, arm in arm with other civil rights marchers. We formed a line of laity and clergy several blocks long and, in search of some transcendence for a secular effort, we all carried candles like the pilgrims in Lourdes. But that march, like my involving work counseling conscientious objectors during the Vietnam War, was ultimately civil in its focus. The religious motives that put me in motion, while based on a common faith, were my own personal motives. They were shared by some of my fellow priests and not shared by others. And we marched or stayed at home in response to these personal, individual readings of our religious sense.

I find this individualism as confidently American as it is intellectually unreflective. We Americans who are so self-conscious in our liturgy that we are embarrassed by the old ladies who unconsciously bob in half genuflections or wave a dampened forefinger before their face and shoulders when they enter a church, we are equally unconscious in our individualism. We American priests speak of authentic religion and genuine faith. But by this we mean only a personalized religious experience. We theologize about the church. As we do so we impose on it an American individualism, seemingly unaware that we, too, are the products of our culture. We become salesmen for American religious individualism because we are so unaware of our prejudices toward institutions and our mistrust of structure. I fear that, in these attitudes, we may be whittling away at the communal foundations of the Catholic Church.

I mentioned earlier that I see the church type of Christian institution, the one founded on St. Paul's image of the church as the Body of Christ, as the one most closely associated with Catholic traditions. This does not mean that the other two views, the sect type and religious individualism, are not a part of traditional Catholicism. They have been, and continue to be, important elements in the life of the church. But they do not have the same social role as the church type.

Religious individualism and the sectarian experience need to make some effective reference to the organic church, the church as Body of Christ. Otherwise they wither, or become institutionalized as an eccentric community living on the fringe of religious society. There they serve little social good and channel most of their energies into a struggle for survival. As I read the history of the church it appears more possible for the roots of a dormant community to send out vital shoots than for the cut-off branches to take root.

The institutional church, in turn, without a prophetic presence will become leaden. The presence of the prophets, who are more concerned with individual rights, with justice, and with the correctness of single issues than with institutional maintenance, and who call the community to account for its moral failings, is vital to the church's integrity. But the prophets and prophetic groups benefit both the institution and themselves when they maintain some contact, strained though it may be, with the church community.

I recognize that these comments betray my own prejudices on the side of the institutional church. Nonetheless I believe that some coming together of the three types of religious institution is beneficial to the well-being of the church. By its very nature, however, this effort at synthesis is a continuing and irresolvable struggle.

The church says it is made up of individuals. It is individuals who enter into the sacraments. It is the individual conscience that is the source of moral judgments. The rights of the individual are clearly defined in the church's theology. And the ultimate good of humankind, the vision of God, is defined as an individual good. (Canon law, founded as it is on Roman law's attempt to defend the state against the unruly individual, is another matter.) The experience of conversion, of turning from one life to a better one and doing what is possible to preserve the integrity of that choice, begins as an individual experience.

Religious individualism and the type of religious experience that is described in the sect view of church are important parts of the Catholic religious experience. But they are parts. They are not adequate, taken in themselves, to carry a communal identity. They cannot, taken alone, define the church. That definition includes these two views, but they must be seen in a living interaction with the communal church, the Body of Christ.

The "church type," in turn, is not an adequate model for the entire church. Seen as a collective body, without making provision for the individual and for the space that an individual needs to function morally, the church becomes totalitarian. To avoid that same totalitarianism the church, in its very self-definition, must make provision for the dynamic processes that the individual goes through in his or her religious life. These processes frequently require an institutionalized tolerance for mobility and change.

This tolerance, in turn, requires an acute understanding of the fundamental difference between ideals and concrete reality. The totalitarianism of the idealist is one of the hallmarks of our age. In the United

States Catholic Church we ascribe the authoritarianism of many pre-Vatican II bishops and clergy to principally Catholic abuses. But their heavyhandedness was part of a much broader phenomenon, one that went beyond questions of authority in the Catholic Church. I can think of two examples of this totalitarianism, each from the writings of a Slavic poet.

In his autobiography, *Native Realm*, Czeslaw Milosz, the Nobel Prize-winning poet, speaks at length of the cultural and political life of his native Poland prior to the Second World War. The church was a strong force in the country, helping to focus the Polish people's national sense. By some it was seen as coextensive with that sense. Religion became an institution for preserving national identity. The individual who turned against one of the institutions, church or state, could be suspected of disloyalty to the other.

After the war Milosz served as a member of Communist Poland's diplomatic mission in Washington and then broke with the Warsaw regime. He draws parallels between political Marxism and the nationalistic and political Catholicism in the Poland of his youth. The totalitarian effect of the two supposedly irreconcilable systems could be much the same. He protests the view that sees the choice of either one or the other as the only alternative, or as inevitable.

In *Doctor Zhivago* Boris Pasternak has the woman Sima lecture Lara in a similar way. But here the choice is between an Old Testament religion that takes precedence over the individual and a Soviet state that does the same. In each situation the community gives the individual his sense of identity and requires of him an allegiance that smothers individuality.

In each of these contexts the individual is diminished. He is a function of a collective. The community not only takes precedence but grasps at and seizes control. The moral person is told to submit to the precedence of the group and is informed that he is at his most moral in that submission. The individual is defined not in virtue of his individualism but in virtue of his belonging to the community. Not only do individual rights begin to disappear, if they do not disappear totally, but the community can persecute individuals, all in the name of fostering the well-being of the community.

The church in America is not exempt from the dangers of this totalitarianism, although its sources are not as aggressive as the nationalism of Eastern Europe. It is more apt to come in the bureaucrat's desire for a neat desk. I have seen that those who mind the store, the bookkeepers and office managers, can be given ecclesiastical authority when the church is viewed as a store and not as the Body of Christ. And then they seek to place people in order and under control as though they were files and figures. There is a heady quality in this power to treat people like things, especially perverse when it is in the hands of men whose disdain for others is as great as the value they place on their own equanimity.

Christian institutions that pursue continuity seem to endure. But that continuity is not enough. For a truly humane life they must also make provision for the mobility of human religious experience, the mobility that is at the heart of the sect type of institution. They must also take religious individualism seriously and make provision for the uniqueness of each person's religious experience within patterns that seem to be common to so many.

I have no illusions about the difficulty involved in what I am suggesting. What can be so easily spoken in theory, as though it involved nothing more complex than mixing the ingredients in a recipe, becomes in the concrete a test of our courage. I am concerned with institutional continuity because twenty years in Berkeley have shown what anti-institutional prejudices can do to the church, to say nothing of civil society. I have seen children raised in our open-ended and neutral society reach adulthood with no means at their disposal to decide and choose other than their own native narcissism and the equally self-serving opinions of their peers.

But I am equally concerned with the rights of the individual. My parents' egalitarianism, family tales of the use of public power for private good, and, I suspect, a culturally Irish anticlericalism have combined to make me wary of the hands that hold power. Four terms of office as a religious superior and the recognition that my own ignorance, whim, pique, or fatigue can impinge on the rights of others has supported this skepticism.

A church which tries to combine the three types of religious institution we have been discussing will do so only because it consciously chooses to do so and continues to make that choice. The tension that is part of holding them together is a difficult tension to tolerate. There will be a tendency to resolve it by moving in any one of the directions embodied in Troeltsch's three types. However, I suspect that when the church has been at its most dynamic it has also been the most willing to make the effort of maintaining the types in a vital tension. And that maintenance, I suspect, can never be institutionalized. Like the effort of a runner going uphill, it is maintained only through conscious, deliberate choice in the face of a strong and understandable desire to let up.

The church into which the convert is initiated is not just a human organization. It is the Body of Christ. To share in the life of the church is to share in the life of Christ, and that is life-giving. It is important, therefore, to make the process of initiation as creative and enlivening as possible. This means that we recognize and draw on the strengths of all parties to the initiation, both individuals and communities.

I recognize that this requires a conscious effort. It is not an effort that can be institutionalized. To say that the three kinds of institution can blend organically is foolish. They come together, where and when they do, only because we make the supremely difficult effort to synthesize them. We succeed only partially in doing so. But then the church is as much a hope to be realized as it is a community in the present.

5

Voluntary Communities

Religion in America is pretty much a middle-of-the-road affair. The blood and thunder, the verve and frenzy, that were the hallmarks of religion in other eras, and remain its hallmarks in other parts of the world, are not a common part of our experience. Yet the appeal and success of cults today, and the occasional catastrophes like the mass suicide of the People's Temple members in Jonestown, indicate that these aberrant situations are not wholly outside the context of American religion. One characteristic they have in common is the importance they place on community life. Since they gain members for their communities through conversion they merit an examination here.

A quality they share, and one which distinguishes them from the organic church of St. Paul's image, is their dependence on the will of their members. This will to belong is often focused on some common issue, experience, or knowledge. They are voluntary communities.

Not all the associations of people in the church are founded on a common faith, a faith which is rooted in the life of a continuing community, and a community whose life is subjected to the scrutiny of critical thinking. There are other groups, voluntary communities, which come together because their adherents choose to have a community in common. From what I can see the organic sense of a community with roots and reasons that go beyond the immediate members is not to be found in a significant way in the voluntary community. The members of the voluntary community are in communion simply because they have chosen to be.

They have made their choice because of a common experience. There is a difference between a common experience and a common faith, at least faith as I understand it within the Catholic tradition. The members of the voluntary community are in a religious communion because their common experience is religious in nature. The fact that it is religious does not change the fact that it is experientially founded rather than faith-founded. And they stay in communion because of their common choice.

Voluntary communities fit into our consideration of the rite of election because they express their appeal to people principally at times of conversion. They also highlight some of the issues that arise in the conversion process. One is the role that critical thinking plays in religious life, an issue we will look into at the end of this chapter. Another issue is the meaning of membership, or the nature of belonging. This issue has surfaced over and over throughout the history of the church. Two ways in which it has surfaced are of special interest because they appear to be increasingly common today. I refer to the movements known historically as gnosticism and antinomianism. Their Greek names witness the antiquity of their origins. I am familiar with them in particularly Californian dress. But I would hazard that our local antinomians and gnostics are true soul mates of their classic counterparts.

For the person coming into the church the meaning of membership may not be important. We join ourselves to others for personal reasons that are subjectively satisfying. My membership in the Dominican Order and my life in the priesthood are more dependent on my own history than on questions of definition. But because our reasons and our individual histories are as varied as we are, encounters between people in the church who take their sense of belonging seriously can surface conflicts about the meaning of membership. The conflicts that swirled around the gnostics and the antinomians are beginning to have a contemporary echoing.

During my first year of study for the priesthood I happened to come upon a repairman working in the chapel of our house of studies. The high Gothic arches and the oak choir stalls had created a very resonant space, and I was attracted to the chapel by the echoing of a slap, slap, slap coming from the inside. When I entered the chapel a strange little man in painter's overalls jumped up from his knees and began patching a crack in the wall. I pretended to pass by. Then I sneaked back, intrigued by this man, and found him back on his knees. He was flipping a metal ruler end over end, apparently measuring the sanctuary. That was the source of the slapping sound I had heard.

He saw me in my habit standing above him and stopped. Then, without looking up, he took out a small notebook and wrote down numbers. Anticipating my question he said by way of explanation, "It is a well-known fact that the secret order of the universe is to be found in the dimensions of sacred space." And then he went back to his patching.

This man was a gnostic. *Gnosis* is the Greek word for knowledge, and a gnostic is someone who believes that salvation can come from the possession of a special knowledge. Usually this comes to mean a secret knowledge open to a select few.

The process of election into the church can have a gnostic quality to it in that there is a concern with communicating the beliefs of the church, and in having the convert receive and learn what it is the church believes. The association of knowledge with membership, and membership into a body that promises salvation, can seem gnostic. Over the centuries there have been gnostic currents in the church. Special revelations, special secret religious practices, the following of visionaries' dictates, come up again and again. And they can, in effect, be gnostic.

But the teaching of Christ was open and public, and intentionally so. The beliefs of the church communicated to the convert at the time of election are the public creeds of the church. And converts are told that the moral quality of their lives is as integral a part of their road to salvation as their faith.

The rite of election takes place during Lent. Lent is a time of prayer, of reform, and especially a time for being aware of God's mercy. At the time of election the focus is on the need that everyone has, both recent convert and lifelong Catholic, for God's mercy. With mercy the central theme of election, the possibly gnostic qualities of the election rite are counterbalanced. For it is made very clear that it is God's mercy that brings salvation ultimately, a mercy shown through bringing people to reform their lives.

Throughout the centuries, however, the church's clear and public emphasis of the central role of mercy has failed to satisfy a recurring thirst for salvation through secret knowledge. This thirst, aberration though it be, crops up again and again. It is satisfied through cults and gnostic movements. It seems to be a part of the human spirit, and consequently an inevitable part of the church's human dimension.

But many people coming into the Catholic Church discover, sooner or later, that the human side of the church can be more human than they had expected or want. What does the convert do when confronted with the church's zealots, inquisitors, and lunatic fringe? In my youth, as I mentioned above, I had the useful stratagem of writing off our parish's two religious fanatics as products of Italian piety. That one was Irish and the other German was not allowed to impeach the stratagem.

One way of coping with this too-human dimension is to withdraw from it. The convert can move into an elitist group. He or she can separate him or herself from the church in its overly human aspects. To do so would not be new, or uncommon. It is a practice that has recurred throughout the history of the church. I want to look at this practice using one of its aspects, antinomianism.

Strictly speaking, antinomianism refers to the belief that the law no longer binds. The followers of this belief interpreted St. Paul's opposition to the old Jewish law as a permission to live without legal restrictions, following only their faith and the promptings of the spirit.

I am not interested in this strict interpretation and will use the word metaphorically. To be more exact, I am not interested in antinomianism, only in some means of focusing the convert's need to come to terms with the peculiarities of some Catholics' piety. Antinomianism has been used in a metaphorical sense to describe those individuals who find the concrete and communal bonds of church society more than they can bear, and so they move into their own, unfleshed church. It is in this sense, with perhaps a cavalier attitude toward accuracy, that I use the word.

Antinomianism on the one hand, and on the other some imagined need to justify the religious practices of all fellow believers, can serve as the extremes within which we can discuss the convert's attitude toward belonging to the Church. Antinomians abstract from the physical.

They are the religious individualist written in totally spiritual terms. "I am a member of my own church, it is a wholly spiritual reality, and I am not in the same world as these others. That they are so earthy and crass is regrettable, but it is not overwhelming for they are wholly other." So speaks our antinomian, or at least our metaphorical antinomian. And he or she probably attends Mass in a monastery, a university chapel, or some place where the physical dimension of so many of the church's unwashed is not evident, or where the communal sense is clearly tenuous.

I suspect that this kind of attitude is a reaction against the other pole, the attitude that dictates a need to justify anything and everything that seems so convincedly pious. The intellectual, the prober, and the connaturally dubious can easily be victimized by this attitude, especially since it speaks to them from within their own souls. It is hard to write off the religious practices of absolutely dedicated and convinced pious people. It is difficult to dismiss them, I suspect, because the converts note the sense of conviction and belonging these people manifest while they themselves feel so much like semiconvinced outsiders.

They see pictures of crowds kneeling before a New York mulberry tree within whose branches a housewife has seen a vision of the Virgin Mary. "What a lot of nonsense," their rational and educated sense says. But some suggestion counters, "God's ways are mysterious." And there is the primal suspicion, "The Spirit often works through the simple." Noting the number of people decorating the mangled branches of the mulberry with rosaries and pictures of saints, the preponderance of evidence begins to fall on their side.

Even more, there is the sense that the faith and the piety of the unquestioningly devout are purer, more genuine, and, albeit maddingly so, closer to the heart of authentic Catholic faith than the patchwork quilt of belief, embarrassment, hope, doubt, and rationalization that mark the faith of the convert. The convert can look at these simple and pious people, recognize that he or she is different from them, but see the difference as a judgment of his or her own religious inferiority.

I find that I have experienced these same reactions on a number of occasions. Perhaps it would be clearer to present them simply as my own. I would do so were it not for the fact that converts also continue to describe them to me as their own.

These reactions, common though they may be, are not good indicators of the truth of genuine Christian piety. It lies in between these extremes of antinomianism and an uncritical acceptance of all that goes by the name of Catholic. Opposing the antinomian's flight from the human community does not entail an uncritical acceptance of that same community. The processes of sound judgment that are valid in the secular context are also valid within the religious context. Using faith for a measure, which we do in the context of revealed truth, does not excuse us from measuring as critically and wisely as is possible.

The need to distinguish the true from the fake, the artistic and the creative from the cheap and tawdry, the maturely and humanely committed from the bigoted or fanatical, is as real a need in the religious context as in the secular. I would say that it is an even greater need in the religious context, for history, as I read it, chronicles the use of religion to justify the fake, the cheap and tawdry, and the bigoted and fanatical.

When we consider that this faith has produced such greatness—here my mind runs from the artistic creations of European Catholicism to the current phenomenal reform of society in Latin America, each a product of a faith seeking authentic expression—we cannot conclude that either the antinomian flight from the concrete into a spiritual world or the uncritical acceptance of all that happens in the name religion is a reasonable course of action.

And yet this same flight from judgment and uncritical acceptance of religious phenomena are as common today as they have ever been. What is their appeal? It is, I suspect, a lack of confidence in reason. Why our supremely human ability should be the subject of such mistrust is hard for me to fathom. And yet it is. Perhaps it is the embarrassment of the ordinary in the presence of the exotic. And human reason, next to the exotic appeals of cults, gnosticisms, or the compelling forces of intellectual absolutism, can seem very ordinary, even dull.

Perhaps we ourselves have to be scarred, or exposed to others scarred by the violence of superstition or absolutism, before we come to appreciate the value of reason. The individual going through the process of conversion can be easy prey to people and movements that capitalize on the limitations of reason. The man or woman moved by the collective and frequently disorderly forces of his or her own human experience to abandon one way of life and to seek another can be victimized by the weavers of magic or the preachers of absolutism.

Conversion is often accompanied by the melting of once firm categories. Where I am going, why I am going there, how I am to get there, were once clear. Now they are not clear. The word confusion means, literally, a melting together. For some it may be liberating, and they leave their pasts freely. But for others it is painful. They can long for the sense of clarity and order they once were able to count on. And it is to them that the merchants of guaranteed directions make their pitch. As I see so often in Berkeley these perfect solutions seem to sell.

Within the voluntary community elected for its provision of support rather than for a valuing of reason, feelings of belonging are substituted for an awareness, perhaps a painful awareness, of individuality. Feelings of warmth (whatever that means; for me it creates an image of people pickling in a tub of warm Rinso) are traded for a sense of moral integrity. The combination, if nothing else, is eminently uncritical.

The late Italian writer Luigi Barzini has stated that it is ritual, not reason, that tames the savage beast in the heart of man. As an advocate of the value to be found in the church's rituals I do not challenge this view. The ritual of election is probably the source of the election process's stabilizing quality. But once the savage beast of dissociation and change has been broken to bridle we must still direct him where we want him to go. For this we need our reason—reason to differentiate between creativity and psychotic dissociation, between legitimate authority and totalitarian power, reason to glean faith from opinion. Perhaps, today, in a world committed to the mastery of technical skills, we most need reason to help us develop the prime human art of making sound ethical judgments.

Our ability to reason may be flawed, but it is the best we have. Alternatives seem all to tend either to fantasies of flight from the realities of human life or to a surrender to one of life's tyrannies. The realization that we can and should approach life critically is one of the greatest benefits that God can endow us with. Few truths are as repeated in our Catholic theology through the centuries as the value of human reason and the need for clear, consistent, and penetrating thought.

Some people choose to enter a voluntary community because their experience in the organic community has been traumatic. They have lost their ability to trust any part of life that is not under their immediate control. So they enter a community whose nature subjects it to the direct control of its current members.

That this choice may not be a humanly free one, as is the situation with some people who act out of their wounds, or is the situation within some cults that appear to coerce or manipulate, is not the point. The community is founded on a choice that has its roots in the experience of the individual members.

The church, on the other hand, while it obviously depends on the will of its members to be members, sees itself as having roots that go beyond immediate needs, immediate experience, and current membership. And it has an ultimate purpose that goes far beyond current issues. The church that existed in the time of Christ, which existed a thousand years later, and which exists today views itself as the same church, and values that sameness. That the living members change over and over is true, and does not change the fact that it is the same church. The continuity is founded on the same foundation as the church itself, Christ. And in light of this foundation the will of the current members becomes only one constituting element rather than the essential one.

6

The Scrutinies

The second part of the rite of election occurs on the third, fourth, and fifth Sundays of Lent. On these days the converts take part in public liturgies, usually within the Mass, that are called the scrutinies. As described in the church's ritual, "the scrutinies are intended to purify the catechumens' minds and hearts, to strengthen them against temptation, to purify their intentions, and to make firm their dedication."

The purification and strengthening touch the convert in very important areas of life. They look forward to the total commitment that will be enacted in the baptismal ceremony at Easter. In this chapter I want to look into three areas in which the commitment of Christian living is made concrete. These areas are possessions, asceticism, and absolutism.

I choose these areas for two reasons. First, they are ones which raise issues that prove troubling to many converts and seek some resolution. Looking into these areas may prove a means to bring that resolution.

Second, they parallel the basic life issues of the church's religious orders, the areas of poverty, chastity, and obedience. Since these areas of the orders' three vows are a symbolic way of articulating the complete commitment that is supposed to be part of religious life, they have been and are the object of much thought. Since they are the object of the vows I myself try to live, I can draw on my own experience as I try to describe them.

Possessions

My mother was born before the turn of the century in a small New Jersey town of clapboard and shingled houses. Its unpaved streets wandered irregularly through pastures and in between stands of chestnut and sassafras trees. The town lay on a newly built line of the Delaware, Lackawanna and Western Railroad Company. In that perspective western meant Buffalo, New York.

The Lackawanna's terminal was in Hoboken, on the very edge of the Hudson River, across from lower Manhattan. Disembarking train passengers were taken across the river on the Lackawanna's fleet of ferryboats. The ferry slips formed part of the terminal, and the boats left every few minutes for the quarter-hour trip to Barclay Street or Christopher Street. Even as late as my own childhood a trip to New York was quite an excursion.

The derelict coaches had woven cane seats polished shiny by years of use. Fine, gritty cinders always covered the alligatored windowsills. They rattled and bounced out of the New Jersey hills and across the empty miles of the Hackensack meadows. Then, slowing to a crawl and jolting sideways every few seconds as we were switched from track to track, we passed through the freight yard walled in on either side by blocks of six-story warehouses. Track gangs of unsmiling, weary Italian immigrants leaning on their shovels and pries—their white-shirted Irish foreman in a different world ten feet away—looked up at us as we passed slowly by.

Arriving in the Hoboken terminal we climbed down from the coach and walked along the narrow passageway past the hot and still smoking engine. Clouds of white steam from a dozen locomotives rose up into the black roof. Mechanics with long-handled hammers walked the length of the trains, striking the wheels to make them ring.

From the tracks we walked to the terminal and then out to the ferry slips. Their entry arches were a Victorian marvel of copper columns, cornices and cupolas, all turned a white green by the harbor's salt. A little boy's desire to stop and stare always lost to the older world's determination to catch the next boat. Past the line of square, chain-drive Railway Express trucks with spoke wheels and solid rubber tires. The waiting truckers in the open cabs joked with the traffic cops who funneled them into the gangway. Dockhands in greasy, high-waisted, brown canvas pants and soft leather caps, kerchiefs tied around their necks, spun the six-foot wooden wheels that lowered and locked the gangway. The cars and trucks bounced over the loose wooden planks, playing them like a dull marimba, while the iron ratchets on the gangway wheels clanked out their own call to hurry on.

Up the canting stairs to the top deck to peer down into the narrow space between the slip and the stern and wait for the black, debris-covered water to turn to white foam, and then hurry to the front. The boat shuddered and began to move, grazing the slip's black-tarred pilings and bouncing the seagulls from their rounded tops. The pilings stretched and groaned, the passengers lurched sideways, the boat slid out into the Hudson, and the seagulls dropped down again onto their perch.

These were the years when America and Europe were linked by fleets of ships. New York newspapers listed their arrivals and departures not as single items but in columns. It was a rare trip on the ferry that did not provide a sight of one of the major liners, broadside in midstream or being nudged near its berth by the red tugs.

The Hoboken waterfront, a crowded and prosperous shipping center a mile and a half across the Hudson from lower Manhattan, held the docks of the Norddeutsch-Lloyd steamship lines. As a consequence many German immigrants landed in Hoboken and settled in the red brick cities on the New Jersey side of the river. Each block of four- and five-story apartments was just like the next, a brownstone doorway to the left and two parlor windows to the right, then three stone-silled windows at each floor up to the corniced roof. They were as square and solid as the people, their churches, their hospitals and schools. These cities with their robust mercantilism and confident, well-run political machines dominated the financial and political life of New Jersey from after the Civil War until the Second World War.

Not all the immigrants, however, wanted the muscular life of these crowded, ethnic cities. Some of them left the security of their German-speaking neighborhoods and boarded the trains to the New Jersey hills and a new life in English-speaking, small-town America. Though only miles from New York, these towns were culturally closer to the Midwest than to the life of the city.

Among those who moved from the city was the family of Willi Meier. Willi was among the small handful of children in my mother's eighth-grade class. His parents were bakers and had decided to open their own business in a new town. Like all bakers they began their workday very early. Getting the day's bread, rolls, and breakfast pastries into and out of the oven in time for early morning delivery was hard work. Willi worked with his parents, an essential helper in their new business and new life. By the time that school began every morning he had already put in several hours' work.

Willi's work was hot and sweaty. The schoolmistress, an archetypal Victorian spinster with a strong sense of classroom decorum and an equally strong sense of smell, decided that Willi offended against each. So she wrote a note to the Meiers and sent it home with Willi. The already overworked family did not need another problem, especially a fake problem created by a schoolteacher. The mother wrote out a stinging reply to the teacher's complaint.

> My Willi ain't no rose. So don't smell him. Learn him! Who do you think you are, Rich?

Nothing that I have read symbolizes for me, or puts so succinctly, the role of money in our society as well as this immigrant baker woman's barb. In our society being rich is not a what, the possessions you have. It is not primarily a how, a means to an end. It is a who. Money is who you are, Rich. In her exasperation Willi's mother scraped away an entire layer of convention to expose one of the West's most basic operating principles.

Over the centuries the church has had to come to terms with many questions about money, poverty, possessions, and the distribution of goods among people. Progressively, the church's leaders have moved from ad hoc decisions to the development of principles. There has been an attempt to make these principles reasonable, consistent, consonant with the teachings of Christ if not based on them, and tested against the reality of human life and human nature. A few of the principles have come from the calm study of religious theoreticians. But most of them have come out of controversies. They have come as answers to difficult and troubling questions that were of major importance to their times.

I want to give an overview of these controversies and the principles that have come out of them. I do so because questions of money and possessions often loom large for people during a religious conversion. The teachings of Jesus and the conscience of the convert frequently come into play around these issues. Furthermore, the questions that occasioned the controversies were frequently converts' questions. So the convert recalling these issues today may feel no stranger to them.

When we look at the church's teachings on money, possessions, and the distribution of wealth, we have to keep some of the facts of history in mind. For example, money is a relatively new concept and a new commodity. The Roman world used money and thought of money not only as a measure of weight for its coins but also as a measure of value. They understood the notion of credit and the idea of borrowing against future productivity. But that use diminished with the shrinking of the empire. In large part the church grew and spread in a world that did not use money. Goods and services were frequently bought using other goods and services in payment. Put simply, people bartered. Money as a government-produced and -controlled means of exchange did not come into general use until a few hundred years ago.

Of course, there were exceptions. During the late Middle Ages the Italian banking cities, such as Florence, Pisa, and Venice, controlled their currency and sold shares in the public debt much as we do today. But within the context of the church's two-thousand-year history money as we know it is a relatively new matter. Since the Church's teachings on money followed its use, which has changed over the years from simple to complex, so the church's teachings have gone from the simple and straightforward to the complex. A view of a few historical high points will indicate how this occurred.

Most of us have heard of the barbarian invasions. I suppose we have images of Huns and Goths riding out of the East, bearded men in leggings and animal skins, with iron spears and shields, their hair long and uncombed. They fall upon Roman towns and villas in the provinces, pillaging and burning as they go. Finally they come to the great city of Rome itself, which they plunder and leave in ruins. It makes a good movie, and there is some truth in it. But it is a partial picture.

What we know as the barbarian invasions can also be seen as mass migrations of poor and hungry people into the lands of the empire. There they hoped to find food and shelter. They can be seen in some way like the mass migrations of the poor from the South of the United States into the cities of the North.

As scholars point out, numbers of the barbarians actually sold themselves into slavery in order to gain the attachment to the land that went with the status of a slave and the guarantee of shelter, food, and some measure of protection that went with attachment to the land.

The Romans were unable to stop these migrations, even though they posted troops on the borderlands at great cost to the imperial treasury. The barbarians came in and, by the force of their numbers, changed the life of the empire.

Their arrival presented the church with real questions. What do we do with them? Are we responsible for them? Can they be baptized? To what extent should we adapt our rites and life to the needs of these unkempt foreigners? The question was made more complex by the fact that most of them were Arian Christians by the time they reached the places where they settled. Arians were early Christian heretics who believed that Christ was more of a hero than God-become-man.

The question of what to do about these barbarians was answered in different ways. Some of the Roman aristocrats, by then Catholic for several generations, had their own answers. "Ignore them. Have to do with them as little as possible. They're illiterate, they're unwashed, and they stink." These aristocrats were not being mindlessly cruel. They were trying to preserve what they could of the cultural heritage of the Greco-Roman world. This preservational role had traditionally been supported by Rome's ancient, polytheistic religion, and the heirs of Roman aristocratic responsibilities thought that the ascendant Catholic Church should now pick up this duty.

But the church sided with the barbarian poor. As long as they renounced their Arian heresy, they could be received into the church. They could take part in the church's worship. They could be married, and according to their own customs. Their laws were to be respected.

Thus a basic principle was early established in the life of the church. The poor and the helpless could look to the church as their refuge and as their protector. This principle has been repeated over and over through the centuries, most notably in recent years by the Latin American bishops' articulation of the church's "preferential option" in favor of the poor.

This attitude toward the barbarian poor can be seen in the lives and writings of church leaders in the first centuries. During this era there was a group of quite extraordinary bishops who deeply influenced the growing church. They were both pastors and writers. They are known today as the Fathers of the Church, and their writings are called patristic writings. They are considered to be an important part of the church's theological, literary, spiritual, and historical heritage. St. Augustine in Africa, St. Iranaeus in France, St. Ambrose in Italy, Sts. Athanasius and John Chrysostom in the Near East, are some of the better-known names. In their extensive writings and recorded sermons we hear the same appeal: show kindness and charity to the poor; open your doors to the hungry and the dispossessed; judge people by their deeds, not their possessions; be honest and do not steal. These are simple, uncomplicated, and thoroughly concrete statements.

There was another patristic teaching that was more ambiguous. The Fathers told their people that while in this world they were really in exile, that their true home was with God, and that their goods should be used with that heavenly home in mind. Christians were to live with a sense of detachment from material goods. As we can imagine, this view did not promote the development of a theology of economics and financial equity.

But by the twelfth and thirteenth centuries the situation had changed. The church was forced to develop answers to questions about money, possessions, and the distribution of wealth because the church and the society it had helped to develop by now had their own extensive possessions. The church also had numbers of converts who wanted to know how to use these possessions in a way consonant with Jesus' teachings about poverty and the Fathers' teachings about detachment. Their situation was new and more complex, and they needed more developed answers.

When Western Europe was divided into Roman provinces it was principally a wilderness. The lands that the barbarians were moving into still showed effects of the ice age. When we think of rural France and Germany, with their rich farms, châteaus, tailored countryside, and an aura of civilization and prosperity that seems timeless we get an incorrect picture. Think, rather, of the wilderness, the swamps and forests, that faced the first settlers coming into America, and add a cold and occasionally severe climate and you have a better picture of early Europe. The church played a very important role in clearing this land, draining the swamps, and turning the forests into farmland.

There were rich and civilized lands in Christendom, but they were around the Mediterranean and especially in the East. Sicily and Spain were productive farmlands. North Africa was especially rich, and a great grain producer. But their influence in the life of the church underwent a devastating change with the rise of Islam. The church in coastal North Africa, which was theologically eminent, was simply annihilated. Spain was conquered by the followers of Muhammad. Sicily was on the frontier, and Byzantium was beleaguered. So the focus of church life shifted to the north. From Constantinople, a city which had a population of several hundred thousand people, the focus shifted to France and Germany, whose "cities" averaged no more than ten thousand inhabitants.

The church was born in the Mediterranean world of rich and cultured nations who prospered from slavery, exploitation, and conquest. The Christian faith of the church's leaders was more a judgment upon the injustice of classical culture than it was an attempt to establish a theory of justice. The church lived in this world, tried to temper its more cruel and predatory aspects, but lived so as not to be overwhelmed by it. As St. Augustine said, Christians were to be citizens of the City of God, not the worldly city. The church's view of possessions was reactionary and charitable, rather than theologically systematic.

The new church of Western Europe was different. Rather than being a newcomer in a long established world the church was often the focal point around which the new world grew. It was a church of monasteries and cathedral chapters. The cathedral chapter was a small community of priests, like a monastery, who served as the bishops' advisers, taught the people religion, and assured the liturgies in the cathedrals. Whereas the monasteries were commonly in rural settings the cathedrals were central points in the cities. Even some monasteries drew communities around them despite their ideal of retreat from the world.

These chapters and monasteries developed religious ideas on possessions and the use of wealth. The teaching came out of their need to make sense of their religious ideal of poverty and the fact that they were accumulating possessions. An example is the notion of the charitable trust. By their vows the monks were not allowed to own anything in their own names. But their education and community life placed them in the position of providing services, such as medical care, for their own members and for some of the people. These services were best assured when institutionalized. From this situation developed the notion of a legal trust.

In addition, it was also a custom for rich men to give nonarable land to the monasteries as an act of penance. The monks received this land also as an act of penance. They would then develop the land, usually swamp or barrens, into farmland. This development was accomplished only with many years of hard work, whence the penitential aspect of the gift.

But with these two practices the chapters and monasteries ended up controlling substantial lands and trusts. The simplicity of living as citizens of the City of God often yielded to the splendor of living as signs of God's power. Some bishops and abbots moved about their territories with horses, retinues, guards, and pomp.

Civil leaders and nobles coveted these lands and their income. They also squabbled among themselves for power, precedence, and jurisdiction. The rivalry for power among all of them, religious and civil, caused frequent disruptions in the lives of ordinary people and left them from time to time without pastoral care of even the most basic kind—such as marriages, baptisms, and burial of the dead. This state of affairs led to cries for reform. It was this reform, only in part successful, that led to the church's theology on possessions and wealth in the Middle Ages.

Some Catholic historians tend to look back to the Middle Ages as a time of faith, of religious unity, and of a principled interaction between the church and the state. I find this view unreal. The Middle Ages were a period of growth and ferment in Europe and consequently in the church. Just as there were many states whose princes vied with one another for supremacy, so there were also the churches of the popes, of the German bishops, of the French and English kings, of the abbots and monasteries, and of the powerful local lords all vying with one another for control and jurisdiction. Among themselves popes, emperors, abbots, bishops, and dukes used force, coercion, interdict, and excommunication to incarnate different ideas about their right to power and jurisdiction. To speak of the state and the church is to think in terms of monolithic structures which simply did not exist except, perhaps, in the hopes of some popes and emperors.

The writings of theologians such as St. Thomas Aquinas could promote the mistaken view that the Middle Ages were a time of tranquillity because the writings speak of faith and social order with no reference to human turmoil. The view of human nature that emerges from them is equally rational. The world is defined as living according to a hierarchy of rationally established principles. Faith and reason coexist in harmony. Reason is as respected as in More's Utopia. Rulers govern with a prudential concern for the common good. Is this a picture of the times? Not at all. Aquinas's writings, for the most part, were never intended to be a picture of the times.

The medieval theologians wrote two kinds of works. One, like the *Summa* of Aquinas, was intentionally abstract, removed from current controversies and even from temporal considerations. It was a matter of definitions, not descriptions. It looked at things the way they exist in the mind, as objects of knowledge, not as concrete realities. Poverty, power, riches, and the use of wealth were defined in the abstract, not pictured as current political and human realities.

From time to time the theologians were also involved in controversies where they were asked to contribute more than definitions. In these controversies they presented their own opinions on what ought to be done. Fortunately, we have a few examples of each method referring to the very same topic, so we can contrast the two methods.

What we know today of the medieval church's teachings on wealth and possessions, teachings that have laid the groundwork for the development of subsequent ideas, is considerable. When taken all together, it seems that these teachings formed an important effort at self-definition. The place of poverty in the life of the church raised questions about the church's identity as basic as those raised by the controversies of the first centuries, and as difficult as those that led to the Reformation. The relevant theological writings are speculative discussions on the nature of justice. But they were, in effect, scholarly discussion papers within a larger and very controversial discussion on the nature of Christian living and the church.

The mainstream of the medieval church concluded that the goods of this world were, indeed, good; that there was, consequently, no virtue in being poor since poverty was the deprivation of a good; and that wealth and possessions were for the benefit of all, to be used reasonably and with an appreciation of human interdependence as a means to help both their owner and the poor have enough for a decent life.

These conclusions have come down to us in a theoretical form, which makes our use of them relatively uncomplicated. But in their origin they were controversial answers to thorny questions. I find it striking that the issues raised seven hundred years ago by Christians trying to make sense of their faith are the same issues raised today by men and women in a similar situation. They are the same issues I myself faced twenty-five years ago. How do we reconcile the idealism so clear in the statements of Jesus with the human need to live in this world? What limits do we put to our acquisition of money? How do we know whether or not any possible limits are valid? Fortunately the minds that grappled with these questions were equal to the task. They had to be, because the issues were raised with a force that anticipated the turmoil of the Reformation.

The medieval reformers fell into two groups. One group followed a dualistic tendency. Spirit was good, flesh was evil; poverty was religious, riches to be spurned; the world and all its attractions the domain of Satan, the realm of God that of spirit, poverty, and unworldliness. With the excess of worldly living on the part of some church leaders it was easy for the advocates of this point of view to gain a following. They are known variously as cathars, or the pure, Manichaeans, and Albigensians.

The other group of reformers came from within the mainstream of the church. They were as severe in their attacks on the worldliness of nobles and clergy as the first group, but they did not follow the dualistic tendencies. The best known are St. Francis of Assisi and St. Dominic. The orders they founded carried on their reform efforts.

The difference between the views of the "pure" and the founders of the religious orders can be seen in the willingness of the latter to be countercultural without wanting to establish a counterculture. Being countercultural involves accepting the goodness of the world as the good that it is, while also recognizing the need to press for reform in those areas where reform is needed. Establishing a counterculture as the Manichaeans and Albigensians tried to do involved them in a rejection of their society, which they saw as essentially corrupt. They attempted to establish a new society founded on different and opposed principles.

Maintaining an intelligent and productive countercultural stance without trying to establish a counterculture is one of the most difficult of challenges. It is especially difficult in religious orders because the orders create their own community and the rules they live by. In effect, they are in a position to create their own world. If they choose to make this world a counterculture they probably have a good chance of making a go of it, at least in the short run. In the long run all countercultures are bound to fail in that, if they endure, they simply become another culture.

I recall that when I first entered the Dominicans it seemed to me that the values we lived by should be more countercultural, and that these values should be institutionalized. In effect, I wanted a counterculture. Greater simplicity of life, more austerity in religious practice, a more single-minded poverty—these were to me the hallmarks of a countercultural life. Like many a recent convert I was prepared to latch on to a readily available, uncomplicated, personal asceticism. With an almost sublime naïveté I also wanted an institution to support that choice and guarantee its probity.

My need for this was real. And the simple and perfect life I wanted was easy to understand. My world had no room for complex intellectual issues and ethical subtleties. In retrospect I marvel at the simplicity and clarity I saw in matters that have perplexed the church for generations. Only with the maturity that comes from years of pastoral experience did I come to realize what is involved in the intelligent weighing of means and ends and an effective working toward those ends.

I do not want to undervalue the convert's need to develop an ascetic attitude toward life. I suspect that the man or woman going through a conversion may well need to bring order in his or her life. To this end ascetic practices can be useful. The need for an order-bringing asceticism can be understood, I find, if we look at one of history's more important and less understood processes. I refer to puritanism.

Puritanism gets a bad press these days, as it has for quite a while. Rather than condemn or defend it I want to explain its function. Put simply, I see it as a middle step, a bridge, from an external morality to an internalized one. Both on the individual level and on the level of society there appears to be a puritanical phase as part of the process of interiorization.

The moral writings of the Middle Ages seem to presuppose a prepuritan society. Aquinas, for example, in those few writings that speak concretely of his contemporaries, sees them doing what is right only because their rulers have the police power to make them behave. In addition to his well-known definitions about moral decision-making —rational choices based on fully understood principles—he described the need to coerce his contemporaries into doing what was right.

For the men in his world these definitional statements did not carry expectations about their concrete actions. Yet they have become expectations for us. We expect that we will act on the basis of principles we understand. This change bespeaks an evolution from an externally directed view of moral choice to an internally directed one. The bridge from the one to the other is the phenomenon we know as puritanism.

The prepuritanical society sees the goods of this world as good. You take what you want and get what you can, because what you want is good and eminently worth having. Property, food, pleasures, and play are to be grasped when and how they can. To keep people from taking what was not theirs or what was not permitted there was the sheriff, the torturer, the jail, and the executioner. Lest their lessons be lost, executions were gruesome, frequent, and public.

With time the level of consciousness was raised and choices became more reflective and personal. We see examples of this in both the Reformation and the Counterreformation. The policing role played by the jail and the hangman were replaced, in part, by a new, internalized view of goods and pleasures. No longer were the goods of the world seen as quite so good. The responsible individual and the morally responsible society need institutional supports. These were to be found in the view that sex is deceptive, pleasure not lasting, many goods not good but evil, and the senses not to be trusted. In short, the view of the puritan.

The puritanical outlook is useful. It gives both the society and the individual an inner resource for coping with instincts and appetites. It is true that the puritan outlook distorts and overstates the situation. It objectifies subjective fears and limitations. It turns subjective fears into moral norms. But it also gives the individual and the society an alternative to external coercion. The puritanical outlook is still coercive. It is not yet rational. But it is inner coercion.

With greater personal or social maturity these strictures are no longer necessary. But their necessity goes away only with maturity. At the time of my conversion and subsequent entry into the Dominicans I imposed on myself an asceticism that was puritanical. The demands of a life of poverty, chastity, and obedience represented a change from the freedom I had granted myself, a freedom limited much more by fear of consequences than by any moral qualm, and I needed unambiguous support. And puritanism is nothing if not self-assured.

Other converts, I suspect, may also straiten themselves within a view of life that distrusts its appeal. This view can have its use for them as it did for me. But since the moral model I am advocating values the supremacy of the individual reason and maintains the goodness of the created order I would hope that other converts could see their ascetic views as a way station on the road to another view. I do not want to suggest what that other view should be, for it is different with everyone. And not having arrived at a fully mature view myself I am not in a position to talk about it from personal experience.

From its social views of wealth and possessions the church moved to a more puritanical view, and thus a more personalized view. Social norms yielded to personal piety and did so at a time when social norms were becoming most needed. As a result the developments of the industrial revolution came face-to-face with a theory of justice that was simply inadequate. Directing the single, pious Christian in matters of detachment and almsgiving was a far cry from the answers required by the size and control of the wealth created from the seventeenth century onward. The need to catch up with social developments was great. The catching up began in the last half of the nineteenth century.

Recognizing the need for a theological system that could address major social questions using principles that were as sophisticated as the Western social system itself, Pope Leo XIII in 1879 reinstituted the study of St. Thomas Aquinas for seminaries. Then, in 1891, he published his monumental encyclical letter *Rerum novarum*. This major position paper on socialism, capitalism, and the condition of the working class began by noting "the enormous fortunes of some few individuals, and the utter poverty of the masses," a fact Leo had seen at first hand during his years as papal ambassador in industrial Belgium. In it he laid the foundations for subsequent social teachings.

The popes of the twentieth century have distinguished themselves by their production of a body of social teaching that parallels social, scientific, and economic developments. Their teachings apply principles of solidarity, the primacy of human needs over profit, and the view that the state and other institutions exist to serve humankind, and not vice versa. Questions of personal piety relative to poverty are seen in the broader context of social needs. And yet, within this social context, the primacy of the individual is maintained. Not only is it wrong to see her or him as a means to an economic or political end, but the right of all people to such benefits as education, health care, decent housing, leisure, and humane working conditions is maintained.

Few issues, I suspect, seem as far from the control of the convert as these questions of social justice. We can all recognize how important they are. But what does one person do about them? I would like to suggest that single individuals really don't do much at all, precisely because they are social, not individual, questions. Recognizing the power and mobilizing the strengths of the social group, and doing this in a nontotalitarian or manipulative way, is one of the major challenges facing the church today. It is especially a challenge in the United States because of the influence of religious individualism.

Asceticism

On an August Sunday in 1957 I drove from the wind-rolled fog of San Francisco across the Golden Gate Bridge into the hot sun of Marin County. I was on my way to one of the most extraordinary years in my life. I was beginning the novitiate year. Newly arrived in California, just a few weeks beyond my own two-year stay in France, I was entering into the world of California religion.

For a year and a half I had lived and studied with French Dominicans who were masters of theology and biblical studies. They were leaders in liturgical renewal. They were the intellectual elite in the church and were laying the groundwork for what would become the church of the Vatican Council.

Père Lagrange, the founder of the École Biblique in Jerusalem and quite possibly the greatest influence on the intellectual life of the church in the twentieth century, had lived and died in this house and was buried in its cemetery. The *Revue Thomiste*, one of the most prestigious of the church's philosophical and theological journals, was published there. The community's liturgy was a conscious, and well-watched, anticipation of the liturgical renewal to come.

There was never any doubt in my mind that I was living with some of the most eminent intellectual leaders of the French Church. From them I picked up the very French and equally Dominican prejudice that life and its course are intelligible. No existentialist angst in those quarters. I was in a community that believed that the world and its events could be understood and shaped by educated men, and I was with them because I shared that same belief.

To me their life was an example of integrity. They lived in a priory, begun in 1295, that is considered a prime example of Provençal Gothic architecture. The cloister, chapel, and refectory, the oldest parts of the priory, are examples of an unornamented simplicity that was typical of Dominican architecture in its first years. Their life was austere because they were poor. And they were poor because their energies went into their studies, their writing, and their preaching both in the cities and to the rural poor. They were disciplined the way that scholars have to be disciplined, and they lived very simply out of a sense of solidarity with the poor in France.

With these austerities there was still a sense of celebration in their lives. On major holidays and feast days the community would gather after dinner beneath the broad stone arches of the *salle du collège*. Cigarettes would be passed out, Cognac or a liqueur opened, and for an hour there would be spirited conversation. With my limited French, on one such occasion, it took me a while to grasp that the topic was the possibility of doing in the cook and disposing of his members through the offices of a local butcher suspected of trading in kidnapped cats from the streets of Marseille.

Their life was integral. The parts fit together. The motions they went through were directed to an end, and the end was worthwhile. To me their life, while austere and personally unattractive because of that austerity, still made sense. The parts came together into a coherent whole.

With this community in mind I entered the novitiate. I knew that religious life would be different from the inside. I never anticipated the source of that difference, for I was entering into a year of mercilessly contradictory images. I was enveloped in the Dominican habit in a symbolic ceremony while the neighbors learned tennis on our courts just outside the chapel. In the hundred-degree heat, with the windows and doors open, we were parts of each other's initiation. *"Veni creator spiritus . . ."* chanted the prior. "Margaret," came the response from the court, "keep that racket straight." As the sweat rolled down my back and thighs and pooled around my knees the five layers of the habit, a Dacron imitation of French serge, were wrapped around and over me to the accompaniment of Gregorian chant and the plop of tennis balls.

We rose before dawn to begin a day spent guarding ourselves from its appeal. We chanted morning prayer in the evening and vespers at noon. We prepared for and performed elaborate liturgies in an empty chapel. We learned of the virtues of detachment and poverty in one of the wealthiest villages in California.

The year in retrospect seems like a Zen experience. It was an encounter with ultimate meaninglessness, survived through ritual and the power of the will. But where Zen expressly attempts to bring order and some sense of harmony into a life that does not have to make sense, Christian monasticism is founded on the belief that life is purposeful. Life is ultimately intelligible because God, who is life itself, is also intelligibility itself.

I was left with the impression that our life was put together by a novice mechanic using a mail-order plan and spare parts. I think of this and recall an incident during a summer I spent in a remote town in Alaska. With summer's heat the tundra softens and becomes impassable. Travel of any distance must be by plane. A metal detector had been installed in the log cabin that served as the town's air terminal. Washington had required it in all airports to stop hijacking, and the locals obviously obeyed government regulations.

One of the town's two policemen was flying out on the same plane as I. The other was operating the newly installed detector. The traveling cop walked through the detector, causing it to screech and squeal. His coworker, obviously startled by the sound, looked him up and down and then pointed to the traveler's waist. "It's probably the gun," he said. So the traveling cop unbuckled his gun belt, handed it to the other half of the police force, walked through the unprotesting detector, and then took the belt and holstered gun back in his hand. "You were right," he said as he buckled his gun back on. "It was the gun."

The hallmark of my novitiate year, as I recall it, was the emphasis on discipline and asceticism. I think of the pattern of asceticism I experienced during the year and I recall the Alaskan incident. We were performing imagined duties that somehow never quite fit into an intelligible whole. We went through all the very same motions I had seen living with the French Dominicans, but here it never really made sense.

Recently I drove by the site of my novitiate. The buildings are gone. Sold, demolished, and replaced with half-million-dollar houses that seem to fit the area more than we ever did. Only the tennis courts remain, the focal point of the new houses and, I imagine, still measuring their players' hopes against their beginnings. I suspect that in these paragraphs I am doing what the contractor did in clearing the land.

I mention this year because the asceticism that was so much a part of it, and especially severe because it seemed to be to no purpose, stands in marked contrast to the asceticism that is asked of the convert. The man or woman coming into the church is asked to bring order into his or her life where that order is needed. It is a means to an end. It is not an end in itself, nor a discipline to be endured as some kind of ritual trial. It is subordinate to the need to bring the convert's way of living into accord with the teachings of Christianity.

One area where there can be a need to establish order is in the expression of aggressive and sexual instincts. Our society is very permissive in matters of sex and, in a more veiled way, in matters of aggression. But what is tolerated by many people is seen as disorderly within the Christian tradition. And the church takes sex and aggression seriously because the sexual and aggressive instincts are so important a part of life and of the relationships that make up our lives. Nonetheless the church's theology on sex and aggression does not always address the questions that face the man or woman coming into the church.

Theologies are produced as answers to questions. Both the questions and the answers are the theologian's. We have to keep in mind that since the end of the first centuries most of the church's theologians have been members of religious orders and were concerned with the questions of the religious orders. The vows of poverty, chastity, and obedience, or their equivalent, are the basic element in the life of the religious orders, so what it means to live them and break them has been described at length. But the place of sex and aggression in the life of a religious with vows is different from their place in the life of the laity. Consequently, the answers developed for the religious situation may well not fit that of the laity all that well.

For example, the matter of aggression and the appropriate uses of power are and always have been major questions in society. But only one aspect of aggression—the meaning of legitimate authority and the right to exercise that authority and command under obedience—became critical both for the church and its religious orders. Consequently, until the church's recent concern with war and nuclear armaments the question of authority was the only one to receive a thorough answer.

Except for a puzzling and relatively recent personal reluctance among American religious to use power, aggression has been seen in a social context. Today the social importance of our aggressive instincts has renewed theological interest in this basic part of life. The church's concern with peace and the limitation of nuclear armaments may well be its principal theological focus. This interest is principally social, not personal.

By contrast, at least since the Middle Ages, sex has been considered within the context of personal behavior more than within a social context. Sex as the object of the vow of chastity is obviously going to be different from sex in the context of married and lay life. The way that sexuality is looked at by someone intending to remain celibate may well be of oblique value to someone with other plans.

The individual coming into the church and seeking to bring order into the area of instinctual expression will be faced with a theology of sex that, in large part, developed with a focus on the individual, and a theology of aggression that is principally social. This focus may not be the most helpful because the convert may have very different questions, such as the proper use of power and ambition in business life.

This context may also raise questions in a way that can move the convert in a narrower focus than is proper. I mention this because I have seen a number of young men and women at the time of their conversion think of entering a religious order. Their interest, it often turns out, lies in the felt need to bring social support to their struggle to live a nonpredatory life. I suspect that they think of religious life in part because the theological models presented to them as rationales for the Christian view of sexuality and aggression were developed as answers to questions on how to live the life of the religious orders. The apparent absoluteness of religious life, more apparent than real, is the other principal reason.

Bringing order to our instincts is an important part of the asceticism asked of the converts. But it is not the only part, or even the principal part. Within Catholic theology matters of the spirit are considered to be more important than matters dealing with the instincts and emotions. So the move from a reliance on self to a reliance on God is considered to be a more important task than ordering the instincts. And the asceticism and discipline that are a part of this spiritual task are more important than the asceticism and discipline needed to develop a control over the instincts.

This point of view even changes the meaning of asceticism and discipline, for it places less emphasis on the effort of the individual and more emphasis on the working of God in the individual. This involves a discipline because it means lessening the sense of control we have in our lives. And this control is one of the chief ways we channel our aggressive instincts. The spiritual asceticism seems to me to be more singularly Christian, whereas the asceticism directed to controlling the instincts could just as easily be found among the Roman Stoics.

The asceticism asked of the convert at the time of the scrutinies is principally a spiritual asceticism. It asks, in effect, that the individual trust God and trust the church. It is a request that individuals trust that the path they have entered onto is not deceptive and, relying more on the ministry of the church and the help of God than on their own resources, they be open to the fact that God is working in them.

The need to develop a control in the area of the instincts may be real. Our society allows much more free rein in this area than do Christian norms, and people coming from a typically secular milieu may well find that their new faith is demanding. But the asceticism developed to cope with these demands should be seen in the context of the more important asceticism, the spiritual asceticism, because order in the instinctual area is ultimately a means to bring greater freedom to the spirit.

Absolutism

Sooner or later a convert will have to come to grips with the absolute. In part this is because God is defined in absolute terms. But also, on the level of our own human experience, conversions bring us face-to-face with ultimate choices. People entering into a conversion often experience a need to take their own state seriously. Sooner or later, they report, they are going to have to make choices. The grays in their lives, or at least some of them, are going to have to become more clearly black and white.

I want to talk about absolutes because mistaking what is and what is not absolute can be a source of pain. Moving from the moral and spiritual relativism of our lives into a Christian life in which there are absolutes can be a disconcerting business. It helps in making this transition to know what is truly absolute so that we do not fall victim to the false absolutes presented to us by our imagination and our emotions. At times of great change in our lives it is common for our emotions and our imagination to present us with imperatives.

I do not recall ever having sought out absolutes. They have always entered my life unbidden. I want to describe these experiences. The examples are diverse, and there is no attempt to assume a pattern in them. They are as diverse as my own experiences.

Very early one morning in Jerusalem, before the sun was up, I dressed and slipped quietly from the house where I was staying. A dozen tape-recorded muezzins were calling out the day's second Allah O Akbar from the loudspeakers of East Jerusalem's mosques, a sound I slept through on most mornings. The members of the Moslem Brotherhood, the early hour seeming to accentuate their already grim intensity, were gathering on the hard dirt facing their mosque as I passed by. Down the Nablus Road, past the Palestinian women unloading their flat baskets of grapes and figs at the Arab bus station, down the stone steps into the Damascus Gate and into the covered arches of the Suq Khan es Zeit.

The noise and humanity of an average day had not yet intruded on the quiet of the early morning. A few Arab merchants were unshuttering their shops, but for the most part the sides of the suq presented an unbroken wall of padlocked metal shutters.

A hundred feet short of the turn that leads to the Church of the Holy Sepulcher a long flight of worn stone steps climbs from the semi-darkness of the suq to the daylight above. The stone paving of an ancient passage, no more than a dozen feet wide, climbs farther between windowless walls to turn abruptly to the right after another hundred feet. Making the turn I walked to a rusted iron door set into the wall. To my dismay it was bolted shut. But I walked a few steps farther on, following the passage as it turned again, and this time found another, larger gate, which was standing open.

I entered into a courtyard centered on a cupola. Like the fancy of a mad architect it had no door, and its windows were covered with screening and bars. To the sides of the high walls surrounding the court were small, whitewashed adobe huts, each with a window and a green-painted door. Several were set facing each other, giving the impression of a street in a small village. Lace-leaved trees and hibiscus added color and softness to the expanse of stone.

Directly in front of me, but a hundred feet beyond the walls of the courtyard and rising large and gray, was the metal dome of the Church of the Holy Sepulcher. I was in one of the most extraordinary enclaves in Jerusalem, the Ethiopian monastery built on the roof of the church.

As I arrived the monks were walking to their small chapel for the Sunday liturgy. Tall, bearded, and black-caped, men whose quiet dignity contrasted with the common bustle so typical in the church below.

Within the chapel a few priests had already begun their chanting. They were behind the iconostasis, and so not visible. A half dozen monks were gathered in the front of the dimly lighted chapel, one of them wearing a medallion and cross, the signs of his office. Near me, in the rear of the chapel, were several men and women. To help cope with the length of the liturgy, long even by Eastern standards, we were given hand-carved ebony staffs which had slightly rounded crossbars at the top. They were designed to permit the user to cross his hands on top of the staff and rest his chin on his hands.

The liturgy had a primitive, fixed quality. Through the semiopened doors in the iconostasis we could see the vested priests circling the altar in procession, carrying incense and ringing bells as they went. They went around the altar as the first Christian pilgrims had marched around the empty tomb of Christ in the Constantinian shrine that once stood beneath us. It was the triple circle, the same one that pilgrims once made around the house of Christ in Capharnaum and that Muslim pilgrims still make today around the Kaaba in Mecca. It was a procession not to be seen but out of reverence for the holy.

One by one the monks in the chapel began the readings in a strained, high-pitched monotone. From behind the altar came a barely audible murmur, like a counterpoint to the sound of the readings. One monk, more learned than the others, stood by the side of the lectern, prompting each of the readers through the more difficult parts of the archaic script. On and on went the chant and litanies, my chin nestling farther down into the crook of my supporting staff.

Several hours into the liturgy, and before the priests had received communion, the consecrated species were brought out in procession from behind the iconostasis into the body of the church. At that point, and startling me no end, the Ethiopians standing near me fell like stones to the floor, their palms and foreheads pressed against the pavement. Their reverence bordered on the abject. And they stayed that way, never daring so much as to look upward, until the receding sounds of the chants and bells indicated that the awesome presence of the absolute, the Body and Blood of Christ, had been removed from the possibility of their sight.

When I went to live with the Dominicans in St. Maximin my own questions about a life choice came along in the baggage. Adjusting to a new country and a new religious sense, and making this effort while struggling to distinguish words in a language that was spoken with the staccato linearity of a ratchet rapping on a cog—none of the peasant mime or Midi ebullience within those reasoned walls—pushed my personal agenda into the background.

But the need to decide what I was going to do with my life did not go away. It came with me when I went for walks into the chalk-white and broken hills of Provence. I was discovering the earth with its colors and fragrance and was being taught by one of the greatest of teachers, the Provençal countryside. Dry and only inches deep, the soil managed to support a fragrant growth. Thyme, lavender, and sage grew along the rocky paths used by flocks of sheep for a thousand years. My boots would crush enough of the growth against their soles to perfume my room for days.

In this country it would have been easy for the grim, gray questions of vocational choice to evaporate into the pure light of the sky. But I was too well schooled in seriousness for this to happen that easily. What was I to do? One thought recurred. I could become a missionary priest. The image of the purposeful, self-confident young American driving a Jeepful of grinning children off to salvation caught my fancy. It was then an appealing image, and it filled the ranks of the Peace Corps a few years later. But it was appealing, not convincing, and I needed to be convinced. There is a sense of the absolute in us and my conversion had brought mine to the surface. I was not about to make a decision affecting my entire life unless the decision could be measured against this absolute, and none of the alternatives measured up.

One thing I did know was that the life of the Dominicans did not attract me. In this rich country they lived in poverty. The evening meal, one night each week with painful regularity, was creamed carrots, then cakes of semolina, or fried eggs. They were poor because they chose the austerity of the scholar's and intellectual's life over that of the middle class, and out of a sense of solidarity with the poor in France.

In a world that valued personal fulfillment their life was built on the self-denial of prayer, and on study, and on publishing. It was disciplined and austere, in some ways even more austere than that of the Trappist monks I had first seen. The monks, at least, had the outlet of hard physical work. But these men were scholars. They spent long hours in study, and in translating that study into usable and publishable form. That they were so influential in the French church and with the French hierarchy and later in the Vatican Council came as no surprise, for the quality of their work was evident.

So was the price they paid. For me that price was determining. The poverty and austerity in their life, and the discipline in their daily routine, was so visible that the rare, hour-long gatherings for coffee and brandy on a major feast day stood out by comparison. But after these gatherings the quiet of the cloister redescended for another afternoon's study, to be broken for the feast day's solemn vespers which were chanted with great attention to the quality of the liturgy. Too demanding, too austere, too intellectual and disciplined for this cozy American who was accustomed to doing what he wanted when he wanted.

But still, I knew that I had to make some decision, and on occasion I would grapple with that need. I was walking up and down in the cloister on one such occasion, alone and in silence, and praying as I walked along. My prayers were, and frequently still are, exasperated monologues. As a theologian I can't help but marvel at this exasperation and the presumption in it that, for some reason, I am owed better. Treating God like the key-holding janitor who is slow in getting the church opened on schedule does not represent the best in the Christian theological tradition.

At some point on this occasion I managed to move beyond this exasperation to something more like surrender. "If you will only tell me what it is I should do," I recall saying, not as a bargain but as a simple fact, "I will do it no matter what it is." At that point it became clear to me that I should become a Dominican, a clarity that has never left.

There was a sense of peacefulness that went with the surrender, if that is what it can be called. The word sounds pretentious, and it is too strong. All that I had done in the process of ending my indecision was recognize that the decision need not be in my hands. And I did not suddenly find that the aspects of the Dominican life that repelled me suddenly became appealing. Quite the contrary. The austerity and discipline I disliked retained, and retain, both their lack of appeal and daily pressure. Nor was the sense of what I should do all that appealing. The life of a Dominican was not something I began to look forward to with pleasure. What the future was was clear, no more than that. There was a sense of rightness rather than duty or obligation, a sense of direction but not one dressed in anticipation or relief.

Sooner or later our belief in God's absoluteness and our awareness of our own lack of that absoluteness come into contrast. The drifting quality that is so real a part of our lives can seem so accentuated by ideas of absoluteness. It is hard to go through a conversion without feeling this contrast at some point. I believe that I experienced it in a way that heightened the lack of direction in my life. For some reason I did not fall victim to the counterfeit direction that Middle America offered with such confidence to my contemporaries. And yet I had none of my own. That lack was, to me, very real.

In the course of a conversion we can experience the need to make a commitment that is absolute. We can feel called to put aside the relativism that is so much a hallmark of our society and, perhaps for the first time, stand for something clear and real. That need can be a very valid one. But within the church we also try to spell out the limits of the response we can make.

God is absolute, we are not. All our actions and decisions are going to be marked by the limitations that are part of being human. To forget this crucial truth can leave us open to the appeal of those people who traffic in absolutes.

We can have a desire for the absolute. We can imagine what it might be like. We can feel attracted by the guarantees and stability promised in the name of absolutes. And there are those who fashion responses to these desires. But they are the weavers of cults. They deal in absolute loyalties, absolute commitments, absolute demands for submission and obedience. And these are all inappropriate in the church.

All that is human is, by definition, limited. Part of the asceticism of the Christian life is that we accept this fact. We live with the need to parse life with the best means we have, our intellect. We can make permanent commitments, but we are stuck with the ability to second-guess what we have done. I find a kind of ontological humiliation in this fact. But living with the truth of our essential limitation is preferable to living in the fantasy that there is an alternative to it.

III

Initiation

"The water was blessed and prepared, the womb of our birth quickened with the symbolic immersion of the paschal candle. Mother Church, Mother Mary. And then there were no more preliminaries; the moment itself had come. I was the first in our group to be baptized. My name was called, and I had to do the now nearly impossibly courageous thing: stand and walk the few paces to the baptismal font. I was as one who in a few seconds will face sure death; there now stood nothing between myself and my meeting with God. I was in his hands now."

FROM JULIE'S ACCOUNT OF
HER SACRAMENTAL INITIATION

JULIE'S STORY

An Account of My Sacramental Initiation into the Catholic Church

Each of the liturgical rites of entry before baptism served as a powerful sign and channel of grace for me. I formally entered the Catholic Church on the feast of Corpus Christi, 1980. This date was chosen more or less as a result of circumstances. The others in my group had become catechumens during the Advent before my conversion. But I can hardly think of a better holy day on which to begin the first stage of my formal entry into the Mystical Body of Christ. When I stood up before the congregation and was signed with the oil of catechumens I knew with that special knowing that God's grace imparts that I was now a member of the Catholic Church, and I was filled with deep joy.

Though we did not take part in any further initiation rites until the first Sunday of the following Lent, March 1981, the first Sunday of Advent was another significant time for me, because I knew now that the greatest part of the long wait was over. The knowledge that we were entering the liturgical year in which we would be baptized filled me with joyous yearning. I looked forward to receiving my Lord in the Holy Eucharist; the day was starting to seem very near and real now.

On the first Sunday of Lent all the catechumens throughout the diocese gathered at the cathedral for the rite of election. There were around three hundred fifty of us. Beforehand, at the parish Mass in the morning, we had signed our baptismal or confirmation names in the church register, an act which meant a great deal to me.

What a sign this great gathering at the cathedral was. People of all races and nationalities, like a microcosm of the universal church herself, converged to give witness to our entry into the church. I will never forget the long opening procession. I was amazed at the great number of converts. It was good to see the wider picture, though I am glad the other rites were done in my own parish, as there is something special about taking these steps within the welcoming family of one's own community. As we all stood in a great circle around the altar to be received by the bishop I looked out over all these multicolored people, and up at the multicolored stained-glass windows which seemed like a continuation of the people below, and felt truly as if we stood before the entire communion of saints, on earth and in heaven.

Lent was a period of trial for me. I wanted to spend this final time before baptism in special preparation, meditating on the basic elements of the faith and examining myself in light of this Christian calling. But I felt at a real loss, with no idea how to begin. Especially toward the beginning I felt real anxiety over whether I should be actively setting a disciplined spiritual schedule for myself (this seemed important to take advantage of this special time, yet I felt a real resistance to doing it) or whether I should relax, let go, and simply trust in the Lord to set his own and work in his own way. I initially sensed that either way, it was to be a time of mortification, of self-emptying, and of dying in order that the Lord might bring me to his resurrection.

Perhaps Satan wanted to trouble me as well for I found myself facing one spiritual crisis after another, in rapid succession. I had to place my trust in the Lord. My faith still needed strengthening or purification and Lent was a real crash course. My godparents were a welcome source of support at this time, as was one of the other catechumens, who had become a close friend.

On the third, fourth, and fifth Sundays of Lent we catechumens went through the scrutinies, a series of public liturgical prayers designed to support and strengthen our faith and help us to weed out what is not of God. Each scrutiny ended with an exorcism and blessing, with a laying on of hands by the priest. Actually, the word scrutiny, which in Latin means a choosing, is misleading in English as there is no element of public confession or examination. Any self-examination is done strictly internally.

The scrutinies were for me a solemn but deeply meaningful process. There was an amazing congruence between the content of the scrutiny prayers each week and my internal, spiritual state at the time. I felt in one sense naked before God and the community, and at the same time I was aware of the tremendous prayerful support the entire community was providing.

In addition to the scrutinies, on the fifth Sunday of Lent we were formally presented with the Nicene Creed. True, we had been saying the creed all along during the Mass, but this presentation highlighted in a special way the core and heritage of our Christian faith. As we stood before the altar reciting the creed I heard the voices of the entire congregation behind us, and this great sea of voices seemed to stretch back to encompass all two thousand years of Christendom, with all of us united in the creed. Words cannot express the deep awe and thankfulness I felt.

As I have said, this was a difficult Lent and during much of it I felt as if I were helplessly floundering. How painfully I discovered that the task of preparation was beyond my own capacity. Then, on Holy Thursday, all of this changed and during the triduum, the final three days before Easter, the Lord himself prepared me in a special way to be united with him through the paschal mysteries.

I took a holiday off from work on Good Friday so that the entire time from Holy Thursday evening through Easter could be wholly centered on God. Throughout these days it was as if ordinary time had ceased to exist; the entire triduum was one proximate preparation for union with Christ, through a reliving of the central events in Christianity.

Holy Thursday began with a modified Seder meal commemorating the Last Supper and showing its roots in the Hebrew Passover and recollections of our flight from Egypt through the Red Sea. The meal and early parts of the Mass, including the readings, were held in a community meeting hall below the church. This was both a social meal and a liturgy. We then all processed up into the church to continue with the Liturgy of the Eucharist, which Jesus instituted on this night before his passion. The Mass had no formal conclusion. Instead all of the consecrated hosts were removed from the church and taken in a solemn procession downstairs to another room where we could remain in silent vigil with our Lord until midnight.

I remained a long time in that room, praying before the Eucharist hidden in the ciborium. I meditated on Jesus' passion, particularly on his agony in the garden of Gethsemane. Lent had been full of distractions, but now I was allowed to sink deeply into the mystery of the death and redemptive sacrifice of our Lord. How greatly I had yearned for this, knowing it to be an important part of baptism.

The tabernacle in the church was left stripped and empty, with its doors wide open. It was a stark shock for me to see it every time I entered the church during those days; a reminder of the Lord's forced removal from among us, this suffering and death. Yet I also knew, with a solemn, thrilling joy, that the next time the Eucharist would be consecrated I would be receiving the Lord in my first communion.

I kept silence during the morning of Good Friday, and then at noon went to the three-hour Good Friday service at our church. There seemed an unspoken bond between all of us, a shared immersion in the Lord's sufferings, which was very beautiful. It was for me a time of true sorrow, but a joyful sorrow.

During the morning of Holy Saturday I sensed a profound quiet, as if the entire world were suspended, empty, waiting. Jesus had died and was not yet risen; all of creation must have participated in this suspension and emptiness on that first Holy Saturday.

It was a cloudy day, with intermittent, gentle rain. Though this fitted the mood, I worried lest the rain spoil the outdoor procession with the Easter fire and paschal candle. I needn't have worried, though. As my godfather reassured me, this had happened many times before: the rain stopped just before the procession and then resumed after we'd safely entered the church.

However, I am getting ahead of my story. First there was the midday rehearsal for us catechumens—a brief "who stands where" runthrough. This was hectic and unsettling, an unpleasant contrast to the quiet recollection of the morning, with the choir rehearsing and everyone running around the church preparing it for Easter. My godmother gave me a medal, a beautiful pendant depicting the Eucharist, which I wore that night and have worn nearly every day since. The afternoon was spent wrapping presents and writing cards to give to the other catechumens. As it began to get dark toward the end of the afternoon, my last afternoon as an unbaptized person, I felt within me an up-welling of light, the anticipation of Christ's resurrection and my own resurrection with him.

After dinner (during which my apartment mate and I spoke only of the most mundane subjects) I showered and put on a white dress I had never worn before, together with some other things that had personal meaning for me. As I walked to the church I experienced a most unusual sensation which I can describe only by using a natural meta-phor. Along the West Coast, a current of cold water from Alaska flows southward along the bottom of the Pacific. During the summer months, however, there is an upwelling of this normally undisturbed water. All the levels of water are churned, to the depths of the ocean, and the waters get mixed.

As I was walking, I felt such an "upwelling," as if every level of my being, every age I had ever been, from earliest childhood to the present was being called up, stirred, awakened. It was the most peculiar, stir-ring sensation. I have never felt anything like it before or since. I felt like a mass of many beings as I walked, some called up to awareness out of an ancient and obscure sleep, and I rejoiced to know that all of me was in readiness, that all of me was to participate in this baptism. Maybe this happens with people who are on their way to meet death, as indeed I was; death and rebirth, as a new being in Christ.

I shall not go into much detail about the great Easter vigil Mass itself. I will only dwell on a few of the highlights. During the long candlelight vigil in the darkened church, the scripture readings un-folded the history of salvation since the beginning of creation. The themes and symbols in these early events all pointed toward that which we now breathlessly awaited, the resurrection of God-become-man from the dead, and our liberation from the bondage of sin and death. All of creation, the whole church, and each of us catechumens person-ally awaited that second crossing of the Red Sea, the death and rebirth into the living Body of Christ.

I must confess it was difficult for me to attend to the homily, know-ing what was to follow. We were called to kneel before the altar as the church called upon the saints for aid in a long and beautiful litany. It may be difficult for anyone who has not experienced baptism as an adult to understand the solemn terror I felt. I knelt, looking up at the great crucifix before the altar, now unveiled for the first time since before Lent and encircled with a crown of shining gold. The congregation was behind us (I was glad at this moment not to be able to see them) and we knelt alone in the sanctuary like small, sacrificial lambs. I felt naked before the immensity of what was about to happen and threw myself with my entire heart upon the mercy of Jesus. As we invoked each saint, I made the most earnest supplication to him or her. I had always loved the litany of the saints. Now, after this night, it is emblazoned in my heart like glowing gold.

After this the Apostles' Creed was read to us in question form ("Do you believe . . ."), and we assented to each article of faith with "I do." How long I had prepared for this, what amazing transformations I had undergone, by the grace of God and the support of the Christian community, to be able to give my full assent to these wild and mighty truths. Each assent was for me like a marriage vow. We then renounced Satan and sin, and again I did so with my whole being.

The water was blessed and prepared, the womb of our birth quickened with the symbolic immersion of the paschal candle. Mother Church, Mother Mary. And then there were no more preliminaries; the moment itself had come. I was the first in our group to be baptized. My name was called, and I had to do the now nearly impossibly courageous thing: stand and walk the few paces to the baptismal font. I was as one who in a few seconds will face sure death; there now stood nothing between myself and my meeting with God. I was in his hands now.

My godparents stood next to me, one on either side, and as I bowed my head over the basin I felt the touch of their hands on my shoulders. I was very glad of their presence, and it flashed briefly through my mind how much this moment meant to them as well. Then I felt and thought nothing more, for my entire being was focused on one act: LISTENING. I was one single unreflecting act of listening as the pastor called me by my new God-hallowed name and baptized me "in the name of the Father, and of the Son, and of the Holy Spirit." I felt the water, simple, real water, running three times over my forehead, and then it was done. I was surprised by how quick it was.

When I straightened up and opened my eyes I saw Father O'Rourke looking into my eyes with an indescribable expression. Oddly I was surprised to see him there, and in fact I blinked at him with that slight social embarrassment one feels when suddenly faced with an unexpected encounter. This was only momentary, for I was also moved by the expression in his eyes and felt great gratitude. But what had I been expecting to see? Perhaps I would have been surprised by anything other than the kingdom of heaven. I think during these brief moments of baptism I was taken out of ordinary time, though I was unaware of time. The experience was not as I had imagined it would be. There was no mystical burst of glory, no consciousness of death and rebirth or great union with God. It was even slightly disappointing. It was so very simple. Yet while I was unconsciously washed clean and reborn a new being I was open like a baby. Just as babies are so simple that they have no self-awareness of their simplicity, no thoughts of this passed through my mind. Perhaps the surprise, though I was unaware of it, was the surprise of returning to earthly time.

After being baptized I knelt again and watched the others as they were baptized, or received fully into the church in the case of the already baptized. As I knelt the immensity of what had happened began to sink in, but it was a knowing rather than a feeling. I knew on some deep, almost inarticulate level that I had been washed clean of all sin, even original sin, that I had died and been reborn in Christ, that I was now a member of the Mystical Body of Christ. I shut my eyes and let this knowing sink in. Yet I did not feel it in the sense of feeling washed or feeling a sense of mystical union. I wondered at this lack of feeling, as I had been expecting it to envelop me as a flood, as some of my spiritual conversions had done in the past. I did not yet know, in those early days, that there are ways of knowing God which transcend one's feelings and can even leave them quite dry.

When we had all been baptized or received into the church we were given a lighted baptismal candle by our godparents and put on white baptismal robes. We then turned and faced the congregation for the first time. What a moment of joy! We embraced the priests, our god-parents, each other, and saw the incredible look of joy mingled with tears in the faces of the congregation. It was with these embraces and the sight of the living body we had just joined, the loving joy shared back and forth between the whole community and ourselves, that the baptism seemed complete. Finally we returned to our pews to begin the final stage of the Mass—the great Eucharistic prayer and communion rite. (I should add one note of clarification. Ordinarily we would also have been confirmed at this point following the baptism. However, as the bishop was coming to our parish on the following Saturday for confirmation we decided to wait.)

My first experiential awareness of my changed state occurred during the Eucharistic prayer. I realized I was in a real way, for the first time, participating in offering the Mass. This experience was intensified when we said the Our Father. It had never occurred to me that it would be any different to say this prayer after than before. Yet Jesus and St. Paul both spoke repeatedly of that very special adoption, and I knew it, the moment I began to say this familiar prayer. With the joyful awe of discovery I knew that God was, in a newly complete way, my Father. I had long known that he was our father in a general way, but now I realized that I and my relationship with him were fundamentally changed. Along with this realization came the awareness that all of us present, and all who had ever been baptized, were united in that same adoption. My voice was blending with the voices of my brothers and sisters, all of us God's children, one family. I know how trite such phrases can sound, but they seem so only because we are usually not able to realize this in its full truth. It was by God's grace the most fitting preparation for my receiving the Eucharist in whom we were all united.

It is funny how off our expectations can be. I had always envisioned that baptism would be an intensely mystical experience, and it turned out to be much simpler. Conversely, I had worried that when I received my first communion I might be unable to see past the external details of eating a wafer of bread. I prepared myself for this possibility by reassuring myself that I had a whole lifetime ahead of me in which the Lord could eventually lead me to experience this communion. As the Eucharist has become so central to my spirituality I was steeling myself against painful disappointment. I was dead wrong here, too.

As the priest prepared the great banquet I kept thinking incredulously that this time we would be partaking. I could hardly believe that after receiving one sacrament I was now about to receive another. I was dazedly aware that this was the most central act of the church, to which we were now finally and immediately to be admitted.

When it came time for us to step up and receive the Lord I felt both timid and brazen. I ask my readers to stop and consider for a moment that receiving our Lord and God, body and soul and divinity, in this wafer and eating him, is the most astoundingly audacious act anyone

could possibly commit! So it was with the utmost timidity, urged on by
the invitation of the Shepherd, that I came forward to receive him.

As I returned to the pew, I saw my godmother looking at me with
one of the most beautiful and tender expressions I have ever seen. In
that look was a gift more precious than any earthly treasure, and it
opened my heart.

We humans are so blessed that though we are creatures like the
plants and animals around us our Lord has chosen to come into us and
fill us with himself in this most intimate communion and transformation. Suffice it to say that on this night I experienced the sweetest and
truest joy I have ever known. Far from being lifted to great heights, I
was very aware of my human littleness, and of what a great difference
there was between my nature and his in this wonderful mingling.

After the Mass there was an informal reception, where we were
joyfully welcomed. There was much laughter, hugging, and gift-giving.
We wandered about in a golden daze and were buoyantly cradled in the
loving joy of the community. In the week before my baptism I had
imagined that this reception would be burdensome, as I expected I
would want nothing more than to pray in solitude. But in fact this
community welcome turned out to be the perfect completion of all
that had gone before.

That night as I slept I woke up many times, and every single time I
woke I was aware of the presence of Christ within me. And then it was
time to go to the Easter Sunday Mass, to receive him again. It was hard
to believe that this incredible, miraculous favor that had been granted
to me the night before was about to be repeated, only one day later.
The thought that I could now receive the Eucharist every day overwhelmed me. Throwing all modern convention aside I wore the baptismal robe to the Easter Mass, feeling at one with those white-robed
neophytes of the ancient church.

That first week, sandwiched between my baptism and confirmation,
was a strange one, set apart from all other weeks in my life. I was like
one who, through a kind of spiritual stroke, had been returned to in-
fancy, unable even to sense or comprehend what had happened to me.
I had an image of a large stone cast deep into a pool of water. The
water looked undisturbed on the surface, for the stone was cast so deep
it sank beyond sight and left no trace. But it was there, sending out
waves below the surface which I knew would eventually spread to the

entire pool of water, producing its effects. And I knew in God's own time the stone would emerge again, gradually becoming more visible to my conscious senses.

I felt like one who had been dazzled and blinded by a great light, the Eucharistic presence of Christ within me, so that everything looked bleached and flat, only partly perceived. All I had known and experienced of our Lord in prayer was washed out. Nor could I meditate on, or even conceive of, the tremendous redemptive mysteries into which I had now been incorporated. No lofty sense of union with the communion of saints in the Mystical Body of Christ. I was like a baby discovering its own toe. I had been reduced to utter simplicity, to begin again. With Mary, now my mother in Christ, I felt as shy as an awkward child.

It was a disconcerting feeling. When I received communion or wanted to make spiritual communion during the day, none of the deep richness of the former relationship unfolded within me. Instead, I was wordlessly aware of this presence within me in this new, utterly simple, and indescribable sense, and that was all. I could not commune with him as an other, a thou. Instead it was as if there were no "me" and "Christ" as separate individuals, so I could not love him in the ways in which I was accustomed. I felt naked.

I was also aware of what a beginner I was on this journey of transformation. The leaven of the Eucharistic Christ was making its first spreading advance in my soul and I had a humbling awareness of how small and ungodly my soul was, how much of this work remained to be done. So I committed myself into his hands. How often this process must be repeated on different levels.

At the same time that I gained an awareness of my soul's poverty I felt freshly light and free from the influence of sin. Far from having the power to drag me down, my sinful tendencies were like little cloud wisps floating across the sky. When I found myself having unkind or prideful thoughts, I simply apologized to the Lord and peacefully turned my gaze back to him again. I knew this lovely state would not last forever, and of course it didn't.

I found that the things which most activated my spiritual awareness during this first week were liturgical prayer, like the Mass and divine office, the Lord's Prayer, receiving Holy Communion, and being with other people. I felt a great desire to reach out to the people around me at work, on the street, and in the church. I was newly aware of our unity in God, so much so that when praying alone and in nonliturgical forms, I felt at a loss.

Within only two days of my baptism I was already beginning to discover that I could pray through Jesus for someone else in his Mystical Body; not just to him, but through and in him. Although it is now difficult for me to remember when I didn't pray in this way, at the time this new awareness seemed revolutionary, and it filled me with humble gratitude and awe.

On the Saturday following our baptism the bishop came to our parish to confirm the high school students, and we were confirmed with them. It was a beautiful experience, and the bishop prepared us with an excellent homily on the Holy Spirit. It was very special to realize that the man who celebrated this Mass and confirmed us with the sacred chrism was a direct descendant in the line of the apostles.

This confirmation was for me a kind of completion, a sealing in the Holy Spirit and bringing to fulfillment, of the sacrament of baptism. I was glad that the course of events enabled us to have a special day focused just on the sacrament of the Holy Spirit. And with this the sacramental process of initiation into the Catholic Church was complete. The long journey was beginning.

7

Sacraments:
The Secular Foundation
of the Sacred

The convert who is preparing to enter into the church through the sacraments of initiation may well be impressed by their otherworldly character. The chances are that, whatever the individual's past experiences, a process like sacramental initiation seems fairly foreign. Whatever world these rites may be native to it is a world other than that of the average American man or woman.

Yet the religious tradition of the church maintains that these rites, which are so central to both the life and the worship of the church, have quite human bases. This does not mean that in their origins they had merely a fortuitous cause, evolving the way that laws and customs develop in any society. Rather it means that the foundations on which they are built, abstracting for the moment from the identity of the builder, are human foundations.

My own ordination to the priesthood, I see in retrospect, paralleled the reception of the convert into the church. I was entering into a public ministry in a way similar to the catechumen's entry into the church. As a way of indicating the human foundations for the sacraments I would like to recall those days.

I was ordained a priest on a gray Saturday morning of June 1962.

The ordination itself required only two hours. But it was the culmination of a series of rites that had begun nine months earlier with solemn profession.

That previous September, after a summer spent in the Cascade Mountains in Oregon, I made the vow which formally and legally committed me to the Dominican Order for the rest of my life. The profession of that vow of obedience took place in a chapel in sight of the San Francisco skyline, just a few days after our return from Oregon. This juxtaposition of locales was important to me, for it highlighted the struggle I was going through, which followed me throughout the process of ordination and set the tone for my first years as a priest.

The summers in Oregon during my student days before ordination were significant times in my life. They stood in sharp contrast to the months I spent studying each year. The summer months were a time of affective nourishment, human support, and the religious orienting which made life during the school year tolerable. The school year itself I experienced as a time of deprivation.

The monastic life of a student preparing for ordination was more than difficult. It was traumatizing. Having had no substantial exposure to religious institutions growing up I had no ready means to evaluate the life demanded of us. We were presented with an institutionalized ideal. I was there out of religious idealism. So I accepted what we were told at face value and forced myself to act in accord with the ideals.

In addition, I was not conscious of the implicit battle of wills woven through the fabric of our formation. My father had set high standards for us, but he also provided the encouragement and support to meet them. He was genuinely proud of our accomplishments. My college teachers, similarly, urged us to excellence by showing us how to achieve it. It never occurred to me to think that things were different in the religious life. That we were being domesticated, broken to bridle and bit like young horses, suggested itself to me only much later.

We lived with prohibitions which, in themselves, had at most a nuisance value. We were not allowed to smoke. We were not allowed to visit friends at home. We were not allowed to have or spend money. But these prohibitions became significant and divisive because my church-schooled fellow students took them with a grain of salt. They had lived with silly, religious prohibitions all their lives and chose to ignore them.

But I, like a few other religious newcomers, observed them not just strictly but scrupulously. During a Saturday afternoon walk in Berkeley my friends, who always seemed to have funds for such occasions, would go into one of the cafés for coffee or something to eat. I would remain outside. I did not have the means to distinguish between what was important and what was not. But neither did my superiors, I feared, for I had seen the heaviness of their hands on the few occasions when these infractions were discovered. And I was afraid of that heavy-handedness.

Had I been schooled in church institutions I would probably have learned that institutional reality and religious ideal are quite different. I certainly had no problem recognizing this in the public area, for I was raised on family stories of convenient relations between police, politicians, and businessmen in New Jersey. But I was trusting to the point of naïveté. While I did not place great confidence in my immediate superiors—they were far too different from the French ideal—I had no experiential framework for judging the authenticity of the life they presented to us. And, as I said, living that life of conflicting values and loyalties was stressful.

I do not think it was simply a matter of an objectively difficult life. Compared with the intellectual competition at Yale and the primitive conditions and poverty of life in St. Maximin, California was a golden land. The stress lay in part in the superiors' use of power. But principally it lay in the affective deprivation and instinctive mistrust of human nature that was part of the ideal they presented.

I did not fight my superiors. I was too afraid of them for that. Afraid of their unpredictability and emotional intensity, afraid of their apparently unresolved attitudes toward the use of power, and afraid of what I judged to be a mercurial use of it. Working briefly in a prison years later I saw the careful, studied actions of powerless prisoners, the ones who belong to no group, have no strong allies, and have no resources to trade. They treat the powerful, be they prisoners or guards, with a civil and fearful distance. That is how I saw my superiors. Give no offense, do what you are told, and stay as far away from them as possible.

Consequently I believe that I learned nothing from them. There was no personal engagement, no locking of horns, no conflict—and no learning. Learning can come through antagonism as well as through acceptance. In my case it did not come because of my choice for distance and uninvolvement.

While I did not openly challenge my superiors I was carrying on an interior battle with the system they presented. In the progressive resolving of that struggle I began to gain the humanizing of my own priesthood. The focal point of that battle lay in the completely different lives we lived during the summers in the mountains and during the school year in our priory.

In the middle fifties a wealthy California oilman had given us his Oregon retreat. It consisted of eighty acres of forest land and a few cabins on the white-water McKenzie River, in the heart of the Cascade Mountains. A complex of large, architecturally creative wood-and-glass buildings was then built along the river front. They were designed exclusively for use by our Dominican students during the summer months and gave no mind to winter cold and snow. The main lodge, a three-story A-frame open to the ceiling, was focused on a fireplace large enough to walk in. Alongside, the architect cantilevered a concrete deck, almost as long as the building itself, out over the rushing river. The construction embodied an almost extravagant attitude of generosity toward the users.

Built into the very structure was an aristocratic sense of leisure. They were designed for collective recreation, for enjoying one another's company on a very human level. They also provided space for quiet and privacy, since each of us had his own room. We chose our rooms on arrival each summer, pulled between choices made difficult only because of their generosity. Did we want to be next to the river's rushing sound, or facing the snow-covered mountains and the morning sun, or quiet and dark deep in the shade of the towering Douglas fir?

Except for our common prayers and meals each day we were effectively free for two months. It was during these months that, for the first time in my life, I got away from the world of intellect and order, competition and discipline. The combination of such amounts of leisure time, friends whom I was learning to trust and love, and this exposure to the earth at its most compellingly elemental was beginning to soften the hard young man I then was.

A few days after I first arrived in Oregon a group of us set out on a five-day backpacking and mountain-climbing trip. Less than a mile into our first day's hike we hit snow on the trail and spent the rest of the day in an exhausting march over melt-pocked, ice-crusted snow. We camped that night in a frozen valley, its three lakes still covered with ice. This was well before the days of frequent backpacking or light equipment, so we were alone in the valley, cooked on an open fire, and simply threw our heavy sleeping bags on the ground. During the night the wind had a hundred different voices as it circled around and around the bleak and frozen valley. And from the ten-thousand-foot peaks the change of seasons set off periodic avalanches that echoed in the cold air.

During the next day's climb of the highest peak, a four-thousand-foot ascent above our camp, a muscle in my leg cramped up painfully. One of my companions, as quiet and gentle as he was strong, climbed down to me and patiently massaged the pain and tightness away. Then he stayed alongside me as we skirted a glacier and moved on to the summit, ready to help again should I need it.

I have forgotten my impression of the view from the summit. I can still recall the look on my friend's face as he turned back to me when I sank in pain on the spine of the mountain. I was not one to put myself in the position of needing someone else's help. Even less was I prepared to see it come with such spontaneity and openhandedness.

How humane and generous were these summers in the mountains, with their hours spent by the river and around the fire, and in discussions that went late into the night. There was none of the summer ministry that is the lot of most theological students today. The concern for such training had not yet come. But there was a schooling in a trusting and hopeful way of living that I find integral to the morally free person. And there was a training in human arts that are essential to a ministry that goes beyond institutional maintenance.

We were schooled in the value of leisure, not in the abstract but by being given leisure. Real leisure can be unsettling, and it was put to bizarre as well as creative uses. One of my classmates, who was not with us for very long, became expert in planning and putting on elaborate high camp tea parties. They were by invitation only, and I was not included. Too grim and disapproving a presence, I suspect, for such fey pastimes.

Initially I spent weeks backpacking in the mountains, always looking for higher camps and trails, the higher above the tree line the better. My mind worked as hard making sense of my new life as my body did in carrying a heavy pack over miles of trails. But even the energetic obsessive can become bored with leisure. It is at that time that it becomes creative. The quiet and emptiness creep in, and in that time of stillness real questions can surface. What am I doing here? What am I going to do with my life? I did not have answers commensurate with the questions.

I contrast the quality of my life during these summer months in Oregon with the way we lived during the school year. The monastic regimen and routine involved an unusual degree of physical proximity. (The day after the mountain-climbing expedition, which I spent alone at our snowbound camp while the others went off to climb another mountain, was the first day I had spent alone in two years.) But along with the physical proximity went very real personal distance. This distance was presented as an ideal. It was also defended very concretely, most notably in a serious prohibition against entering each other's rooms, a prohibition that had to it all the feel of a taboo as well as the knowledge that disobeying it would spell real trouble.

The community structures either grouped us all together in very public places, where relations were formalized, or separated us one from the other, each into his own private world. But the separation was not for the sake of personal or intellectual privacy. It was clearly a defense against intimacy.

Exposure to the radically different life of our summer months could not but create conflict. How could the same order be presenting us with such divergent views? Which view of the church and of religious life was authentic? With the insistence on clarity that can come so easily to a young man I wanted these questions answered unequivocally. The more deeply I came to experience and understand the two views the greater the conflict became.

Lest its significance be lost on me I had a powerful reminder close at hand. William Everson, a leading poet in San Francisco's post-World War II Beat Generation, was then a member of the Dominicans using the name Brother Antoninus. He lived in our community and was a strong influence in my life. Rather than patronize me or try to talk me out of my questions he sharpened them. At the time he was reading the works of Carl Jung, and he used the categories of Jung to explain religious life. He fed fuel to the conflict growing in me by describing the ways a life that institutionalizes distance and formalism can become deadening, and he illustrated his ideas by pointing to specific individuals, for me a sobering emphasis.

A tall, gaunt, severe presence who peered at me intently and, so I assumed, with devastating comprehension, he was even further increased in stature in my eyes by his association with the most creative and well-known artists in the Bay Area.

"My God," he roared out with laughter the first time I took my questions to him, "a mind, a mind behind that scrubbed and polished Irish face!" Hardly a response to put me at ease. But he helped me understand that my conflict was both real and was one only I could resolve.

How does the private person relate to the public role? "I think I want to be a priest," I told him, "but I don't see that as involving some common image. In fact," I insisted, "I have a real aversion to clerical stereotypes." From him I wanted to find out how a man keeps his spirit alive and active when trying to live a life that for others proves to be deadening. I was thinking of life in the priesthood in my question, but I have since realized that I was also speaking as one of my own generation.

He gave me no direct answers. But he did help me connect my questions with the Christian spiritual tradition. The other side of the coin that demands clear, unequivocal answers is the suspicion that there are no answers. So I was content to be answerless. It was enough to know that my questions were the right ones.

It was in this state, then, that I made my solemn vow of obedience and prepared for ordination. I had just returned from nearly three months in Oregon, months during which I had time to think about the events and life that awaited me on my return. I was, of course, free to leave and to return to lay life. My temporary vow was expiring, and with it the obligations that the Dominicans and I had to each other. But there was never any question of that in my mind. And my community and superiors had unanimously approved me for solemn profession. Further, they decided that I would be ordained to the priesthood in June of that same year, an unusually short period of time after profession. For me the question whether or not to be ordained was not a major issue. I had made that decision at the time I entered the order. For me the question was how to make that religious commitment personally humane and religiously authentic.

In church teaching the priesthood is seen as having different degrees or stages. Deacons, priests, and bishops are seen as sharing to different degrees in the one, same priesthood, that of Christ. During the Middle Ages, when the place of worship in the life of the community began to be seen in a very ritualized context, other church offices were viewed as stepping-stones to the priesthood. To distinguish them from the office of deacon, priest, and bishop, which were called major orders, the other functions were labeled minor orders. They have either been restored as lay functions or deemphasized since Vatican II. But they served as important steps in the move to the priesthood for me, for they initiated us into a sacral dimension in a compelling way.

The first rite, the tonsure, was not an ordination at all, properly speaking. It was described as constituting us as clerics, a legal not a religious category, and was defined in legal terms. But the rite itself was far from a legal formality. As it remains today in Buddhism it was for me a powerful and affecting ceremony.

We rose, the five of us, well before dawn, scrubbed ourselves shiny, got into our black suits and Roman collars, and with our white habits in a little satchel we drove into San Francisco. At the old St. Mary's Cathedral, a Victorian brick pile that would have warmed the eclectic heart of John Ruskin, we met the bishop. He was to give us the tonsure during his 7 A.M. Mass.

We changed quickly into our habits and took our places in the sanctuary. This bishop, we were told, liked things done with little ceremony and with dispatch, and we were not to keep him waiting. Ordinations then were performed on one of the days of penance and fasting that came up four times a year, days whose Masses already had long readings, and we weren't to make things even longer. The people at Mass had to get to work, he had to get to his breakfast and his day, and, like the long readings, we were a religious obligation to be endured. How many hundreds of times had he been through this?

Nonetheless it was powerful. I went and knelt at his feet as he sat on a faldstool before the main altar. He took a scissors, a dull one such as children use in kindergarten, and cut five uneven lops of hair, in the shape of a cross, from the top of my head. As he did so we recited, phrase by phrase in Latin, first he then I repeating, lines from the Psalms. "God, you are my lot and my patrimony. It is you who restores my heritage to me." The last Latin word, *mihi*, he pronounced in a San

Francisco-colored seminary Latin "mickey." I repeated with a Latin by then colored by my studies in France "meehee." He looked at me and then corrected himself, "Meehee."

After Mass, at breakfast in his cathedral rectory dining room, he was jovial and hospitable, instructing his willing cook to "give these fellows a decent breakfast for once." But the joviality notwithstanding we were being set aside. Lest I have any doubts of it, for the next few weeks I lived with the stares of startled people on the street who wondered why that young man had those irregular patches of white scalp showing in the midst of his brown hair.

Four other ordinations followed, two for the minor orders of acolyte, exorcist, lector, and doorkeeper, then one for the subdiaconate and one for the diaconate. All highly ritualized, all at the crack of dawn, the sense of seriousness and gravity increasing with each. The subdiaconate and, especially, the diaconate were involving because of the responsibilities that went with them, and the clearly sacramental character of the diaconate.

Today it is common to fault the sacral, ritual character of Catholic liturgy prior to the Vatican II reforms. The individual, it is argued, was lost within magic rites. I find the argument inadequate. It is true that who I was as an individual and the very different, personal histories of each of my classmates entered into our ordination in no way. To the contrary, we were vested in a uniform manner and treated alike. Had there been one more or less of us it would not have changed the ordination in any way.

Today there is a concern with individualizing and personalizing the priesthood. But that process presupposes that we possess it in the first place. In the teaching of the Catholic Church that possession comes only by the sacrament of holy orders. The symbolic actions of the bishop, principally the action of laying his outstretched hands on the head of the person being ordained, so the church teaches, actually gives the priestly power. The sacraments are seen as sacred signs, but signs which actually bring about what is being signified.

In this sacrament we were given a public office, a significant public role in the church. But, as with the newly baptized, there is also a need to appropriate this role. For the most part we were left on our own to figure out how to join ourselves to that role.

I know from experience that it is possible to help those preparing for ordination and the newly ordained learn the art of "going public." But it is not an art easily learned. For it is not like taking on a public, elective office for a limited time. Learning a job, even a significant, public one, still allows the distinction between the person and the work. The sacramental life of the Christian, be it that of the baptized or the ordained, is different. It presupposes an integrity, a congruence of the human parts, that comes only with effort, time, and some awareness that the person is engaged in an all-involving, serious, personal struggle.

Today it is common in our American ordination ceremonies to personalize the rite in a way which belies this reality. I am not talking about the narcissism and triumphalist bad taste that now and then mark an ordination. Rather, I refer to the more common, deliberate playing down of the archetypal and impersonal dimension of the priesthood, and an emphasis on the personal. It is as though the integration of the two, the public office and the person, has already taken place. But the struggles that the newly ordained continue to experience in their first ministries suggest that this integration does not come readily. I see no advantage in pretending that it does.

The equally adult convert is told at baptism that the need for integration and further growth is still real. In fact, the last of the rite of initiation's four stages is established to meet this very need. There is no expectation that the convert fake it and pretend to a maturity and experience in living the Christian life that is not yet there.

Catholic tradition maintains that the sacred and the secular are continuous. The holy and the sacred build on a very human, secular foundation. But this belief developed in part in a polemic context, in opposition to those who preached a clear dualism of spirit and flesh, light and darkness, sacred and secular.

The church's belief in the secular foundation of the sacred does not mean that the continuity is an easy one. In the concrete the integration of the two is as much a hope to be realized as part of the Christian life, and realized with much personal effort, as it is a current reality. But it is a hope built on the potential congruence of the two, rather than their basic opposition.

In retrospect I am impressed with the sense of passivity that marked my ordination. I did very little. What took place was done to me. I recall thinking of the lamb being led to the slaughter, but thought that

that was bad casting on all sides. I remember only fragments of the ceremony. Walking in slow procession with the bishop into the filled cathedral as the lighted candle clenched unsteadily in my right hand spilled hot wax onto my fist; the bishop anointing my hands and then someone binding them together with linen bands—there were a number of faceless attendants throughout the rite; kneeling before him as he placed his hands on my head in the act of ordination itself.

I think I had a sense of reverence toward what was going on. But it was not a happy or joyful occasion, a fact that does not trouble me in the least. The sense of responsibility and some faint glimmer of the extent of the commitment I was entering into crowded out almost all other responses. And my own natural introversion made me uncomfortable with all this public attention. If nothing else my ordination proves that the process of building the sacred on a secular foundation can be quite a construct indeed.

It is also helpful for me to see the process of my ordination in the context of the times. My years in France, my summers in Oregon, and an interest in my own inner life were also an aristocratic distancing of myself from the major political issues of the time. Typical member of the silent generation, I was more concerned with the affective side of my life, and with the friendship and domesticity of the religious life, than with the ministry. Anticipating the sixties somewhat, I was involved in my own personal growth and for five years wrote down and analyzed my dreams under the Jungian direction of Antoninus. In some ways I suspect that what my college classmates were doing by distancing themselves from the world of work in the affluent, good life of the suburbs I was trying to reproduce, but in my case it was transformed into a religious context.

At least one part of me moved in this direction. Then there was another part, the prober and reformer and religious idealist. It was this side that was brought into the ascendancy by the process of ordination. The ritual of ordination was moving me effectively back into the world of social reality and into the world of major social issues. The very ritual was making me go public in a way that, left to my own introverted, intellectual nature, I would never have chosen. Because of the ordination and its initiation into public ministry it was only a short step into social and political involvement, and away from the concern with domesticity that marked so many of my contemporaries. That this involvement in the issues of the day accompanied an abandonment of the ritual and transcendent was, I see in retrospect, understandable but unfortunate. We were not unable to live with the stress that was essential to keeping them in uneasy balance, we were unwilling.

I was fortunate in that Brother Antoninus had drawn a small number of people to the chapel of our house of studies as their religious center. They were an intellectual and artistic group, an unusual combination of personal fragility and deep wells of strength. Some of them were converts working hard to pass for natives. Others were born Catholics trying somehow to reconcile the weight and symbols of two thousand years with their own needs for creative freedom. They came occasionally to Mass, commonly to compline, the ancient night prayer of the church which we chanted in Latin at nine o'clock each night. They lived on the margin of social acceptability and were frequently poor and often in need of help. It was with them that I experienced my first real ministry. In a time when most priests were dealing with institutional maintenance I was presented with questions of faith, disbelief, suffering, and an almost palpable desire for hope and transcendence.

Their needs were often as great as the trauma in their lives was overwhelming. The hospital emergency room, the juvenile hall, and the courtroom were as central a point to my work as the church office where, more commonly, the priest carries out his ministry.

Despite the difficulty I experienced in responding to such basic questions, despite the stress that was their daily lot, and despite my discomfort facing public institutions like the court and the hospital in a Roman collar, for my own sense of pastoral inadequacy and unpreparedness was as strong as my lack of identity with American clericalism, I had no questions about the value of the work I was doing. If there has been any bridge in my life for connecting the secular and the sacred, and for actually bringing them to the point of integration, it has been my work with the marginal and the powerless. Once again this reinforces my belief that the continuity between the two, the sacred and the secular, is tenuous, and almost violent in its union.

What is true in single instances also appears to be true in the order of time itself. Here, too, the bridge is a forced one. The Catholic Church has survived the passage of time in part because it established some of its institutional life outside of time. In its Latin liturgy, in the intentionally abstract quality of its theology, in the symbols of authority used since the early Middle Ages, the church attempted to add a note of timelessness to its self-view.

As part of this task of self-definition, which faces any group of people, the Catholic Church has said that the essentials of its life and nature are not subject to the erosions of time and the changes in custom which affect other groups. History, of course, can narrate the series of changes that have, in fact, taken place in the life of the church, even ones brought about by causes as insubstantial as fad and fashion. But since religious institutions exist principally for their own members this self-view of timelessness still remains significant to the people of the church.

In October of 1966 I joined ten other Dominicans in establishing the first Catholic community at what was becoming Berkeley's Graduate Theological Union. It was an extraordinary event because it represented a change in this important self-definition, from timelessness to involvement in change. Today seminary education, in an ecumenical context and in conjunction with a university very much involved with the life of the country, is becoming so commonplace that we take it for granted. It is hard to recall why we experienced such a sense of transformation and why this event brought on such feelings of elation. It is not easy now to review the full-page coverage in the New York *Times* and in *Newsweek* with anything approaching the sense of awe that I felt that day.

This pioneering event was correctly perceived as the radical change it was because it represented a major change in Catholic institutional life. Hans Küng was in Berkeley that day and cited the founding of our community as a concrete example of the future church he had come to describe. Seminaries are more than schools for training of priests. They are also statements in self-definition. They are mirrors held up to the church's beliefs about the way things ought to be. And they are both symbolic prizes and strategic territories, fought over by contending parties to show either their legitimacy or their ascendancy.

For this reason our struggle and success in establishing the Berkeley community was significant. Not only were we successful in establishing a new direction in seminary education, but we exchanged some of our participation in the extratemporality of traditional religious life for a greater involvement in religious reform and political action. Had I known the extent of that exchange I would have approached it with greater awe.

I know it is common to talk about blending the sacred and the secular in comfortable union. Perhaps it is possible. But it is not common. The strengths of the church have come to the fore as much in the pursuit of each of these, even as extremes, as in the pursuit of a balance between them. The church lives in large part by symbols, and there seems little benefit in symbolizing the commonplace.

I recall an ordination to the priesthood during my life in St. Maximin. One of those ordained was a Carthusian monk, a member of perhaps the strictest and most ascetic order of hermits in the church. He was from a monastery in a remote valley in the Provençal hills north of Marseille. Their secluded life was protected from intrusion on three sides by chalk-white cliffs that fell abruptly from the ridge to the valley floor. A solid stone wall, set among oak trees, guarded the fourth side. In this valley, walled off by both people and nature from the world, each of the monks lived alone in his hermitage consisting of a workshop equipped with primitive woodworking tools (whose products would never be put to any use), a simply furnished oratory, and perched above under the red tiled roof a small bedroom of spartan simplicity. Food was delivered from the kitchen twice a day and left outside each door. Once a week, after the Sunday Mass, they ate in the common refectory and then went for a walk in their atypically shaded Provençal valley. *"Oui,"* said the prior in quiet understatement, *"c'est spéciale, notre vocation."*

The prior and the young deacon arrived the night before the ordination and went to their rooms. They came by the evening bus from Marseille, which passed over the mountains not too far from the monastery. They went to the chapel for the midmorning ordination, to the refectory for the postordination lunch, smiling but saying little and eating only the vegetables, and then excused themselves. They took the early afternoon bus in order to be back at the Carthusian monastery for vespers.

An event comparable to a wedding in the degree of celebration and festivity usually associated with it was sandwiched in between the evening and afternoon bus. Precious little balance between the sacred and the secular in this event. As I saw the young priest in his heavy white woolen habit board the bus and the door shut behind him I had an image of the monastery door also closing behind him, perhaps for the last time in his life.

Ten years later I sat with a group of Dominicans in an old brick house off East Capitol Avenue in Washington. They were discussing the establishment of a community in this house they were renting temporarily. That part of Washington was then solidly black ghetto. Just a few blocks away were the shells of the buildings burned only months before in the riots following the assassination of Dr. Martin Luther King. The men in the community were concerned with social change and were working in poverty law, in civil rights legislation, and as prison chaplains. Their life and their work was set completely within the context of American life in the middle sixties. Where they would be five years from now, even one or two, they wouldn't ask. Their neighbors were living from hand to mouth and from day to day. The neighbors' rights, supposedly guaranteed by law, were more like privileges to be withdrawn at will. A terrible war was in progress, swallowing up thousands and thousands of lives. In this context a concern with the future seemed almost indecent.

Again, in this situation there was little balance between the sacred and the secular. My friends were as committed to the realities of the moment as the Carthusian was to the reality of timelessness. And each was doing so for the very same religious motives. The church, it seems, is as willing to support these prophetic extremes as it is to speak in favor of a balance between them.

Time and timelessness, concrete reality and wild romance, they are bridged over and held together in the sacraments. And that bridge, as tenuous as it may be, forms a functioning union that has the ability to transform our lives.

The converts who present themselves for the sacraments of baptism, confirmation, and the Eucharist stand before the altar much as I and my ordination classmates stood before the altar at the time we became priests. Sacramental initiation has a common quality to it. Ritual, by its very nature, casts a robe of uniformity on its participants. And even if all the converts do not wear the prescribed white robes there is still a sense of commonality in which they share.

Obviously they come, each of them, from histories as personal and individual as my own. I have spoken of the process of my own ordination at some length because the conversion that preceded it and the preparations that led to it parallel the sacraments of initiation. And I have described the human side of this process because it is through these human elements, necessarily concrete and individual in every case, that the sacred is made manifest.

The scriptural readings for the Easter vigil, the nighttime rite during which the converts are received into the church, speak of several passages. From the first pages of the Bible they speak of the initial passage from chaos and nonbeing into order and existence. They go on to speak of the passage from slavery to liberation, and from sinfulness to freedom from sin. They speak of the change from a life lived with a heart of stone to living with a human heart.

There are more readings for this rite than for any other liturgy in the church. Implicit in this variety is the recognition that the individual histories of the converts being baptized, like the collective history of the race and the church, cannot be expressed in any one, simple way. There are too many truths, too many facets to a single life, let alone a people's history, to admit of a single or summary explanation.

The actual rite of initiation is more symbolic than personal. The rite uses very concrete elements—water for the baptism, sacred chrism for the anointing in confirmation, and bread and wine for the Eucharist. But the rite sidesteps the concrete elements in the histories of the individuals being initiated. The individualism of each person is not ignored. Rather it is preserved under a common mantle of entrance which recognizes the diversity of origin, the similarity of goal, and a personalized latitude in reaching that goal. Each one reaches a common goal, but in an uncommon and individual way.

It strikes me that this lack of individual focus is necessary to preserve the freedom and integrity of the individual. Initiating an individual, as individual, as we do in our social structures today, and as we religious do today in our religious orders, is not a transforming ritual but a battle of wills. Today, the individual in secular society commonly wins the battle. In our religious orders one of the prime lessons taught the novice is that he or she cannot have things his or her way. Communicating this lesson is viewed as a major task by our formation personnel. But in either case, the secular and the religious, the victor in the battle ultimately is battle itself.

The male ego slips easily from a lesson in spiritual obedience to a battle of wills. I have learned from my own experience in the ministry, most of which I have spent as a religious or ministerial superior, how readily American men regress to a primitive competitiveness. In this struggle each ends up saying, in effect, "I will have my way." And the male ego is never quite as close to the diabolic, I suspect, as when it squares off with another human and says "I will have my way with you."

The church's rites of initiation and ordination avoid this destructive struggle. They do so by speaking definitionally rather than volitionally. And they depersonalize the encounter between the candidates for initiation or ordination and the celebrant. There is, for example, a major difference in having the ordaining bishop, commonly the new priests' own bishop, ask them "Do you promise respect and obedience to me and my successors?" which is the actual question, and looking them in the eye and asking "Will you obey me?"

In his treatise on faith, the faith that is professed at the time of initiation, St. Thomas Aquinas says that faith is an act of the mind, not of the will. It is intellectual rather than voluntary, a matter of knowledge, not will. I believe that this intellectualism can be seen in an even broader context. If the mind is the chief means available to humankind to seek out God, then a struggle of wills has no place in that seeking. The primitive man with the club in his hand, the king with the sword in his, and the religious leader with the Bible or code of law in his, all seeking through coercion to have their will with others, have no place in the religious context. They are all kin to one another and essentially different from the religious leader who presents truths and a life goal to the conscience of the individual.

The rite of initiation is a way of presenting this goal to the convert's conscience. Rite appears to orient the person, leaving the mind free to grapple with questions of faith without entering into a struggle for power. In the course of the rite of initiation the convert is asked if he or she believes. That impersonal question leaves much more room for personal freedom than the personal encounter which seeks to coerce the individual into professing a belief.

8

The Role of Worship

In the spring of 1957, during my student days in Paris, I made a pilgrimage from Paris to Chartres. This pilgrimage was not some extraordinary personal piety on my part but an annual event organized by the students at the Sorbonne. Because of the numbers taking part—some twelve thousand of us—we were divided into two weekend groups. For me the event was memorable. Seeing that much religious interest, even mere curiosity, alive in such an attractive group of young men and women was impressive. But even more impressive were our two liturgies, the two Masses celebrated during the course of our march.

The first took place on a field in the Beauce, the great rich plain that for centuries has been the granary for the Île-de-France. As the sun began to set we gathered, all six thousand of us, on the slopes of a gently indented fallow field. Off in the distance, its twin spires standing gray in the soft evening light, was the great cathedral that would be our goal the next day. We had marched all afternoon from the special trains that brought us through the suburbs southwest of Paris and let us out within striking distance of Chartres. In our compartment, by way of introduction we presented our reasons for taking part and commented on the sense of expectation that hit us all as we saw the immense crowds of students moving toward and into the Gare Montparnasse.

The afternoon had been, by turns, rainy, windy, sunny, windy, hail-punctuated, and sunny again. We had marched through farm villages, chanting the rosary set to a rather uninteresting modern plainsong, while the farmers looked on in apparent incredulity at this strange invasion. Bundled against the hail and rain, stripping off wet layers before the sun, and stretching out on the grass for occasional rest periods, we finally reached the little town that was our goal and were billeted in the barns of willing *propriétaires*. From there we walked to the place of the evening's Mass.

Set up in the middle of the field, to my eyes a marvel both of engineering and of preparation, was a large and imposing canvas canopy. Its four corners were fixed tightly to well-anchored poles that pointed up and outward. The softness of the white fabric, which arched down slightly in the center and between each of the canted pylons, contrasted with the sharp angularity of the supports and their taut steel cables. Beneath the canopy was a broad, square platform surmounted by the altar for the Mass. Six lighted candles, bright enough to command attention in the twilight, were set in front of the altar.

This altar was the visual center of our liturgy. But even more, the liturgy was our center. It was somehow clear to all of us that what was going on in this Mass was the focal point of our pilgrimage. This Mass, with its excellent contemporary music and commanding sense of drama, was as well fixed in the vitality of our youth as the now black spires silhouetted against the last light of evening were fixed in the life of the Middle Ages.

We were divided into sections of about twenty-five students, and each section of students had its chaplain. The priests accompanying us had come from all regions of France. Our section's chaplain was a professor from the seminary in Strasbourg, an alert and quick-minded intellectual. He had met with us several times at the Centre Richelieu, the Catholic student center at the University of Paris, and had helped us articulate what it was we each hoped to gain from the forthcoming pilgrimage. He had also brought to our small group a sense of our own participation in the church at large through our participation in the liturgy. One of the priests on the staff of the Centre, Father Lustiger, a young man newly ordained and a convert from Judaism, had told us that many of the priests accompanying us led hard lives in de-Christianized country villages or industrial slums and were with us as much to benefit from the vitality of our faith as to bring us the strength of their own.

Most of the priests wore their black cassocks during the march. The roughness of their hiking boots and the varied styles and colors in jackets contrasted with the stiff formality of the cassocks. Just before the liturgy began they each put on a white surplice over the black cassock, and in the process signaled for me a shift into a sacral role. The presence of all these priests gave me a sense of continuity both with the religious history of the country and the spiritual values which, for me, they actually did represent. At communion time they each received a ciborium of consecrated altar breads from the main celebrant, a Parisian bishop, and moved out into the crowd accompanied by torch-bearing acolytes.

The sense of unity that bound us all together was founded in this liturgy. And the liturgy itself was an expression of the common faith of the church. It would be an exaggeration to say that everyone there shared in that faith, or that the unity was somehow all-pervading. The motives were as diverse as the faith of the young men and women there. But even then I was able to understand, in some beginning and inarticulate way, that that liturgy with the faith as its foundation is the hallmark of the church.

The following day, after we reached Chartres, we gathered for a Mass celebrated by the bishop of Chartres assisted by a half dozen other bishops and our own priests. It was clear simply from looking at their faces that these leaders of the French church were deeply moved by the thousands of students gathered in the cathedral. And for me the bishop of this historic cathedral city, large blue fleur-de-lis embroidered on his flowing white vestments, bridged the years between the time of the cathedral's founding and the present.

Allied to this sense of participating in a continuing history I had some awareness, perhaps for the first time, of what is meant by a religious people. Taking part in a Mass sung by six thousand young voices in this magnificent church gave me a real experience of a believing community. There was more there than the sum of the parts.

There was a community, a people. Faith in this context is not just a personal belief, a function of isolated individuals. It is also a part of the society, and an essential, basic part at that. And it is within this understanding of faith that we look for the Catholic notion of worship. Worship begins in this context of a public, social faith and reaches its perfection there as well.

Here the teaching of the Catholic Church differs from the belief of churches in other traditions. In the Catholic belief the faith of the church comes out of the community at worship. The living body of believing people, gathered in God's name and with God's guidance, proclaims its faith in God. This proclamation is the starting point for all theology and all other religious teaching. The theologians in the church do no more than take the faith of the people and put it in orderly form, develop it, and defend it. But they do not create it. In the sequence of causes their work follows upon the faith expressed by the people at worship.

In some churches in the reformed tradition the opposite is true. They come together in virtue of a commonly agreed on statement, or covenant. They are covenanted churches, as their names often indicate. The founders, in effect, agree on a statement of faith, the people accept it, and their community is the result of that articulation, presentation, and acceptance.

But in the Catholic tradition the church itself is prior to any statement of faith because the church is seen as the Body of Christ present in this world. And membership in the church involves faith in an organic way. Faith is a quality of the person and is concomitant with belonging to the church. But to grasp the Catholic notion of faith we first have to understand the communal, organic notion of belonging to the church. We belong to the church not as we would to a club or a social group, by agreeing to follow the rules and pay the dues, but in the way that the branches are a part of the tree.

For this reason St. Thomas Aquinas, using what to our ears are the unusual categories of medieval theology, asks the question whether faith is principally an act of the intellect or an act of the will, and he answers that it is an act of the intellect. Translated into our times this is a way of saying that our faith does not bring about our membership in the church but is more a recognition that we already belong. Faced with the question "Is all this business about Jesus' life and death and resurrection, and the Catholic understanding of the church—is all this true?" the convert has the ability to answer "Yes" and mean it. That is the understanding of faith as an act of the intellect. It is seen as a God-given ability to see a truth not visible to human eyes.

For this reason the presence among the believing on our pilgrimage of young men and women who were not sure what they believed was not a problem. The church was not asking them to submit—"Will you accept what we tell you"—but something very different: "Do you believe this to be true?" Their ability to say yes was a gift of God, not an act of human submission. And those unable to answer yes would not be faulted for this inability but encouraged to remain close to the church as to a vital source.

The church's liturgy, principally the Mass, is a vital source of faith because it has elements which nourish that organic sense of belonging. It begins with a reading of the scripture. Hearing these stories of our human struggle to reach God, the common failure in these efforts, and God's compassionate actions in coming to us instead has been a source of faith for me and for others. It builds up to the reception of the Eucharist, both literally and symbolically an act of nourishing. The liturgy is social and that in itself is, for many, a very real source of strength in faith. While any quality of person, like faith, obviously values the person, faith in the Catholic understanding also clearly recognizes the collective roots for that personal quality.

I value and appreciate this organic understanding of faith and membership in the church because it has been so important to me. Having been raised in a family that was both Catholic and anticlerical, I find it both helpful and accurate to separate questions of faith from questions of submission and obedience. They are simply not the same. Whether we liked or respected the clergy saying the Mass on Sunday did not change the fact that it was still a Mass that we were attending.

I recall being told by my mother about the first church in our town. It had been established at my grandmother's insistence and came out of a confrontation between her and the archbishop of Newark. Concerned that there was no Mass for the Italian immigrants working for my grandfather, nor religious instruction for their children, she arranged for an Italian priest to come out from Newark for Sunday Mass. These arrangements, of course, were made without involving the local pastor or the archbishop. They were very busy men, she pointed out, not always practical, and need not be bothered about local matters. Translated, that meant that they might not have the ability to see the absolute wisdom in everything she did and were best kept uninformed.

After moving out from Brooklyn in the years following the Civil War my grandparents had been accustomed to go in to St. Peter's Church in Belleville, six or seven miles away. It was an old Gothic brownstone with a cemetery alongside where my great-grandparents were buried. Then after 1880 they went to the new church in Nutley, a few miles closer. But hitching up the horse for the hour-long ride seemed an unnecessary effort when there was a priest coming to town. The Mass said by Father Pietro Catalani was just as much a Mass as the one in their parish church. He might be Italian but, as Mama pointed out to anyone benighted enough to miss the obvious, he was also in town.

In addition, he didn't come alone. He brought with him a nun to teach catechism. Mama decided that the nun who came to teach the Italian children could also teach her own children. The woman was the superior at the newly established orphanage, was well known for her work in setting up hospitals and orphanages, and, Mama concluded, obviously bright enough to read the catechism. Since she and the priest came to Sunday dinner there was no reason why she couldn't prepare the children for their confirmation while Mama was preparing "better than she'd be getting with the nuns." Mama, as my mother recalled, was very practical.

This mixing of Irish and Italians didn't go over all that well with everyone. Some of the locals were not about to attend a Mass said by "Dago Pete" and made sure that the Irish pastor in Nutley heard that his turf was being invaded. When Mama showed up at the cathedral in Newark for the confirmation ceremony, her own and the Italian children in tow, the archbishop stood up before the ceremony and announced that he would confirm the Italian children. But the Irish children were to go back to their own parish and he would confirm them when he got there and not before.

Mama's recounting of what happened next was interspersed by Papa's exclaiming at every phrase "Good God, woman, you did what!" "I stood up and I walked up to the front of the church. But the archbishop ran out into the sacristy. So I opened up the gate in the altar railing and followed him out there. He asked me what I wanted. I was very respectful, considering. I knelt down and kissed his ring and told him, 'Your Grace, we must have our own church, for if we don't our children will lose their faith.' And he said, 'Very well, Mrs. Woods, you can have your church.' "

The kitchen in my grandparents' house was the center of family life, and the large Gothic clock was its chief ornament. But the new church, which the people were going to build when Mama had raised the money, would need a tabernacle. The kitchen clock was sacrificed for the tabernacle. Papa carefully removed all the working parts so there was nothing left but the elaborate shell. And then Mama took her white satin wedding dress, which she had been saving since her marriage, and cut it up to line the clock.

This strong sense of involvement in the church, even in the local parish, was not related to the clergy. My uncles, who had sent their sons to Lawrenceville and Princeton rather than to Catholic schools, were accused of a breach of fealty. When one of them died none of the local clergy would say his funeral Mass. To show his disapproval the pastor brought in an Italian priest from Newark for the Mass, little realizing the precedent for his actions.

While ungracious, these failings of the clergy in no way affected our sense of being Catholic. We were Catholic because of our faith, not because of our clergy. We were members of the church in virtue of our baptism, not in virtue of our relations with the priests. And while we might have wanted more gracious clergy, who they were and how they lived did not affect our belonging to the church, because that belonging was antecedent and organic. There was no covenant between us and the people of the parish, nor between us and the clergy. What we were was members of the same church.

In my Dominican Order we are all quite clear that what is primary in our lives is our faith and our membership in the church. Our order exists with the approval of the church in order to serve the church. We are not another church. We have our own constitutions, true enough, which give form to our communities and our life. And perhaps these could be seen as analogous to the covenant found in other traditions. But our own laws are quite secondary to our membership in the church. And our coming together in the liturgy, which is Catholic, not Dominican, is more basic to our life of faith than our coming together in those things that are proper to our membership in the order.

Catholic worship cannot be understood outside the context of faith.

Granted, there is a ritual base to our worship that has nothing to do with faith. Ritual has a human foundation and is a creation of the human spirit. It is also true that there is nothing essentially Catholic or Christian to many of the more eye-catching traditions that people commonly associate with the life of the church—artistic life, priesthood, monastic traditions, charitable institutions, ascetic practices. These are all part of the secular foundation of the sacred. But what we have built on these foundations we have done because of our Christian faith and in order to express our faith.

I think of those two liturgies in the spring of 1957 because they stand out in my mind as examples of an entire community, a people, at worship. But they also capture the pilgrim nature of the church, a church as much made of people not quite sure where they are religiously as it is home to the subjectively certain. In that crowd of six thousand, and within the much smaller group of my own friends, were people there for a variety of reasons. Some were there out of a deep, personalized belief, surprisingly deep in students as young as we, others because boyfriends or girlfriends were Catholic and present. There were the religiously wandering and the merely curious.

Yet they were there. And, with the hindsight of a priest and pastor, I am glad they were there. Were they there as believers? I don't know, and some of them, I knew well, didn't know either. But looking at their situation from a Catholic understanding of faith we would rather have them there than not, for it is in the context of that believing people that faith comes about.

The worship of the church is not a filter, separating the elect from the rest. It presupposes faith, but it also gives rise to faith and nourishes those whose faith is not that strong. The theologians of the church deal with this apparent contradiction by saying that the church's worship is both cause and effect. It is effect in that it presupposes the faith of the believing community. And it is cause in that it also gives rise to faith in people who have little or no faith. Within this typically abstract, almost clinically antiseptic statement is a human reality that involves groping and uncertainty as well as the belief that certainty is also possible and real. This statement about worship as both cause and effect is also the theologian's way of saying that community is more important than certainty.

The liturgy recognizes that there is the certitude of faith, and that people move to that certitude. It recognizes election, ritualizes it, and gives it a public and religious prominence. But it does so within the context of a pilgrim church, not a triumphant one. Just as the church in its worship is not elitist, so it does not express its faith as a means to exclude.

The church's liturgists have come up with a definition of worship which they find useful because it applies as well to the Mass today as it does to worship in the time of Moses. They speak of a calling together of God's people, in God's name, by one set over the community by God, in order to hear the word of God and offer sacrifice. This explanation was designed, again following upon the fact of the community at worship, not defining it, because it fits the celebration of the liturgy as well in a church in Middle America as it does the worship of Moses and the Israelites in the desert of Sinai.

Again, this shows the theologian's attempt to come up with a rationale that is useful in explaining the life of the believing community to that community and others. But the explanation presupposes that community. The rationale comes out of the community, it does not create it. The theory is adapted to fit the believing people, not the other way around, because faith is essentially a quality of people, not a set of propositions.

The final aspect of worship I want to examine is ritual. The man or woman being baptized or received into the church at the Easter vigil is in the middle of a believing community. But entrance into that community is not only personal. It is highly ritualized, with a ritual dating back to the first days of the church and common to the entire church.

As I noted above, the Italian writer Luigi Barzini said that it is not reason but ritual that tames the savage beast in the human heart. Bringing our elemental forces in line with Christian values is an obvious part of the conversion process, and I find that Barzini's observation probably addresses ritual's most important function.

Earlier I described how the process of my own ordination to the priesthood was not only subjectively powerful but effective as well in the way it transmitted to me a sense of public identity and responsibility. Ritual plays a major role, in fact the major role, in the Catholic tradition of worship. And since it is liturgy that is the hallmark of the Catholic Church we cannot understand the church and its worship without some understanding of the function of ritual. This is a difficult task under the best of circumstances, simply because the matter is so complex. It is especially difficult today because we have so little sympathy for ritual.

Anthropologist Mary Douglas, who has studied the role of ritual in both primitive and urban cultures, notes that ritual has fallen on bad days in the church. The word ritual is often equated with meaningless ritual. What carries meaning is not ritual but the conscious, deliberate, and willed actions of the participants. In the religious sphere this means anti-institutional religious individualism. Sociologist Robert Bellah supports this observation and adds that "our individualism . . . cannot even comprehend the social ontology of the church."[*]

The church's sacramental worship is built on rituals that not only carry meaning but involve causality. It is the belief of the church that through the action of the priest, for example in the sacrament of the Eucharist, the bread and wine become the Body and Blood of Christ. The man and woman do become no longer two but one through their marrying each other, and the convert does become a member of Christ through the sacraments of initiation—baptism, confirmation, and the Eucharist. Whatever the sources of ritual in the human psyche, and whatever the forces in our history that have shaped its development, it has made its way into Catholic worship in a significant and central role.

Barzini's contention that ritual has a taming function is supported by a broad range of disciplines. Sigmund Freud maintained that there is an antagonism between human instinct and culture which is mediated by symbolic processes. No matter whether we agree or disagree with his view that this antagonism is biologically founded and irreconcilable, it does seem an accurate observation that it is the rituals of a culture that direct instincts into socially acceptable patterns. This ritualized directing, as Freud suggested, also seems to be preconscious.

Anthropologist Douglas, on the other hand, maintains that the perception of symbols in general is socially, not personally, determined. Different societies at different times have greater and lesser abilities to make use of the symbolic, and our society happens to have a diminished ability.[†] Unlike many today she is troubled not at all by the magical and wryly distinguishes the sacramental (ours) from the magical (theirs). Societies with more functioning ritualism are able to social-

---

[*] *Commonweal,* December 3, 1982, p. 653.
[†] *Natural Symbols,* New York: Pantheon, 1973, p. 9.

ize their citizens more successfully, a principle she maintains is as true in the streets of London as it is in the forest paths of New Guinea.

The idea that ritual is principally a means of socialization is basic to my own view of it. No matter whether we are speaking of the youngster moving from a state of dependence and insignificance into socially acceptable individuality, as Freud does, or the established adult moving into membership in the church, as the rite of initiation does, we are speaking of socialization. And we recognize that the individual has the capacity to choose to live as a member of the community as well as the capacity to rebel against it, even violently and destructively.

Historian Christopher Lasch, if I read him correctly, sees ritual functioning in family life in much the same way that Douglas sees ritual functioning in religion. Our society has consciously worked to replace the effective role of the parents in the process of socializing children with child-rearing by experts. But, as Lasch points out, combining nurturing and disciplining in the same parent, as we once did, required that the child come to terms with her or his own sexual and aggressive instincts through the symbolic process of learning to live with these parents. Taking these functions from the parents, or separating them, deprives the child of the opportunity to socialize these instincts in a way that is personally strengthening.

Our society with its religious individualism, its equation of consciousness with authentic religion, and its mistrust of socialization by structure has, as a consequence, a culturally diminished capacity to appreciate symbols and a religious prejudice against ritual. Do we have anything going for us that will allow us to appreciate ritual? Yes, we have the life of the church, a life that is symbolic in a broad and inclusive sense. And, I believe, we still have some rituals that are commonly used in the church which have the power to move us.

The life of a vital parish community can be seen as a symbol. I think of my years as a pastor and I recall how the efforts of people in service to one another proved transforming to those who served. Old women overcoming culturally instilled and personal reticence to bring communion regularly to invalided elderly found in that effort a deepening of their own faith and, surprisingly enough, a clearer sense of their own identity as Catholics. From the fringe of social authority in which women of their generation saw their place in the church, they moved to a place where they now speak as the representatives of the church.

Being of service was not new to any of them. They had all spent their lives taking care of others and were expert in it. But having a ritually delegated sacral role, and a ritual functioning in that role, was new.

I think of ordinary Catholics serving as sponsors to converts going through the rite of initiation. In the months or years of the sponsorship they discover that their sense of belonging is heightened. The same can be said of married couples who prepare engaged couples for marriage. In these instances the common element seems to be the assumption of a significant, ritualized public role involving ministry to others. Their efforts prove transforming to them in the way that symbols are described, for example by Jung, as transforming.

In many an American Catholic parish sacramental preparation is in the hands of religious educators. These educators are formed not in the sacred sciences, which seek to understand the faith at its deepest, but in religious education and pedagogy, which are more concerned with methods of instruction. By sheer force of numbers, a force supported by the uniformity to be found in religious formation, education rather than worship is becoming the hallmark of the typical American parish. And it is education understood as preparation for an individualist, personal-growth-focused, affectively rather than intellectually directed life. Nor is it education seen as preparation for ethical decision-making, which would require more intellectual preparation than is often available to the educators.

Within this educational context the sacraments are seen as culminating an educational process. Under this influence many parishes treat the rite of Christian initiation as an educational program capped off by a concluding ceremony. It is not seen as a causative ritual, i.e., a sacrament, that can benefit from teaching. The difference is crucial.

There can be a religion which has no faith, be it a formalized "pop" brand of contemporary Christianity or a Latin distillate of centuries of religious culture. But it is hard for me to think of a vital Christian faith which has no religion, at least faith understood in the Catholic tradition. For the Catholic tradition is so incarnated, so much a part of the world and the flesh, that a faith separated from these is not a part of human life. Faith is a human quality and is shaped by human life. And it is so that it may give further shape and direction to human life.

IV

Mystagogia

"Since my baptism my sense of the church has changed. Before my baptism, and before my own confrontation with the limits of faith, I could take both faith and the church for granted. I had done so years before, during my first tour through the Renaissance cities of Italy. The church was just one of life's imperatives, like the buildings in New York or the communities of impoverished outside Mexico City—a physical presence with no moral dimensions. That's easy to do when you're an outsider looking at the church as one more part of life, an eternal institution powered by the spiritual struggles of others. But I can no longer afford that luxury. Now that it is a part of me I can see how dependent we are on each other."

FROM EDMUND'S ACCOUNT OF HIS LIFE
FOLLOWING HIS SACRAMENTAL INITIATION

EDMUND'S STORY

*An Account
of My Life in the Church
Following upon My Sacramental Initiation*

I became a Catholic on the twenty-fifth of March. I can still recall the date, and I recall it because it was a wonderful experience, and very different from what I had been expecting. I don't know what it was I had been expecting, probably the kind of sober ceremony I associated with state religion. But instead of burying a national leader or crowning a pope, this rite would lead to my baptism and confirmation.

It would be burdensome, I imagined, something that I would simply have to endure. The preceding period of Lenten preparation and the neophyte's dutiful attention to the old pastor's homilies on self-denial had established this anticipation. It was confirmed by the handsome young associate pastor, who tried to sound optimistically Californian but only sounded hollow. My mind's association of religion with penance, and my own recognition that I needed to get my life in order, saw to it that the weight of the rite would not be unexpected.

To my surprise it was very different. It was a wonderful experience. I was nervous, I recall, but even more, I was excited. After initial hesitation I had told my few Catholic friends that I was to be received into the church. I had planned to do it all very quietly, like some necessary but unseemly task. But then I found myself talking about it. Religion to me, when I had thought about it, seemed essentially personal and private. So I was surprised at the way I went and told them that I was going to be baptized and invited them to come to the baptism. They seemed pleased with my decision, even the ones who didn't go to church very often, and they did come to the ceremony.

My family was not religious. My father had been raised by a religiously strict father who forced him to go to church. Father reacted against this discipline, and when he got out on his own he simply cut any church ties. When he began dating my mother he was pleased that she, like him, had no religious encumbrances. Needless to say we belonged to no church.

When I first came in contact with the church I had what then were common American ideas about Catholics. They are narrow, I thought, they are religiously strict, and they are very concerned with obeying rules. For some reason I also thought that because they were religious they were not happy people.

Looking back, I can see that these views were the ideas my parents had about their own religious backgrounds. They had nothing to do with Catholics. But we were still sufficiently identified with our abandoned heritage that we wanted it to appear worthy of us. The Catholic Church, I parroted, was so foreign. In fact, it was the church's eminently American success, and the fear that we might be replaced by it, that caused us such concern. My parents had rejected their religion but they were still closely associated with the institutions it had begotten. So there was a real sense of loss when I became a Catholic. It was as though I were no longer a part of them.

Like most of my friends I had become familiar with the worship of the different Christian churches in our part of the country. When I went away to college in a city with a large Catholic population I had the opportunity to see more of the church at first hand. I found that Catholic worship, the liturgy, actually appealed to me. Of course I didn't believe any of it, but as a creation of the human spirit I found that it had a powerful attraction, an attraction that was both new and strong. And there things remained for many years.

A few years ago, when events in my life made me start sorting out my beliefs, I found that the church was closer to the beliefs I discovered I had than I had anticipated. It was certainly closer than any other church to my own developing beliefs. I think, in retrospect, that I had always believed in God in some intuitive way. But I was not a Christian.

But there came a time when I found that I had to recognize what I did and did not believe. These are things, I suppose, that we prefer not to have to think about because they are frightening. There are times when simply getting through the day can be painful, and we can pray, "Oh, please help me get through this." That prayer, for me, is comforting. But we can reach a point in these prayers where we really begin to wonder, "Is there really something or someone there, or am I just going through these motions because it is comforting? Does this praying mean anything, or does it just make me feel good?" For me these questions were frightening and unsettling because by then I had realized that praying—at least this kind of emergency call for help—was comforting and did make me feel good. But I also wanted to think that my prayers, whatever they were, made some sense.

I knew that my wanting it to be so did not make it so. Either there was someone at the other end of my prayers or there wasn't. And then matters clarified sufficiently to take the edge off my doubts. I had no enlightening experience. Rather, it was more a sense of affirmation which I attribute to my participation in the church's worship, the liturgy. For me the liturgy is affirming. I would leave the church assured that there was a God who heard our prayers. But it took a while for this confidence to extend to the church itself.

After I entered the church I thought of myself as a Catholic, and I willed myself to be a Catholic, but I didn't feel like a Catholic. It was as though I had emigrated to a new land—Australia, or Kenya, Oz even—and knew that I had to start acting like a citizen. But it was an effort and, in part, an act. I would attend Mass, I would go through the ritual motions and do so consistently, but with more loyalty than ease.

I would read the newspaper headlines about statements coming from the bishops or actions coming out of the Vatican, and I would find myself reading with apprehension. Had they done something that would put the church in a bad light? Was something being said without taking into account its effect in the press? Looking back I think I was wondering if they were going to do or say something to take my new life, my new faith and commitment, and crumple them like a paper cup.

It's strange that my faith could have seemed so fragile. And yet those anxieties and fears were real. During those same early months I made a trip to New York and on Sunday went to an early Mass in a church near our hotel. It turned to be some kind of Slavic church. The priest, old and dark and caving in under the weight of his years, went through the motions of the liturgy with a kind of fixed formality. The explosive, forceful sound of the language made the Mass sound like a gentle scolding. His congregation, mostly old women who were occupied with their beads, interrupted their prayers to make the ritual responses and then went back to their rosaries. Of course I understood none of it, and was even unable to identify the particular Slavic language. Yet the foreign feel of the liturgy brought with it none of the apprehension I felt in reading of the church in the newspaper. I could cope with the institutionalized aspect of church life. It was what people might do with it that I found unsettling.

It also seems that there are some people who are naturally religious. They move to faith easily. It seems to complement their temperament the way that the desert flora complement the heat of summer. They are equally optimistic. They look at the world around them and, like God in Genesis, can say that it is good. I find an example of this in Tennessee Williams' trust in the goodness of human passion.

Then there are others, like me, who reach this conclusion only by an act of faith. Left to our own we would conclude that there is little in life to lead to that hopeful judgment. My own experience tells me that we are a race of sexual predators. I moved beyond this view not by natural disposition but only by faith, a faith that came at great personal cost.

My faith's need for strengthening, or perhaps it was a need for purification, became most evident in the fall of the year. Then, as each year began to come to an end, as the summer's life died and the rains of winter fell cold and dark, I found myself following the year's course. Was there anything more to life than this repeated cycle of life that blooms for a short while only to die and rot away?

The death of an old friend during a particularly forbidding December storm, a friend who had no religious belief, no hope for an afterlife, heightened this fear. She wanted me with her in her final hours not to offer comfort or hope but only to ease the pain of lying on the edge of annihilation.

Afterward I sat for a while in the hospital lobby, doing I don't know what exactly, other than postponing my need to leave for the last time. I left by the emergency entrance because my car was parked nearby and the rain was falling hard. Immediately adjacent to the ambulance dock two men in black were wheeling out a long, brown box toward their hearse. The box was made of waxed corrugated cardboard, the very essence of economic efficiency. My friend had left instructions that her body was to be cremated immediately after death. There was to be no funeral, no memorial. "What are your preferences for disposal of the ashes?" the undertaker had asked. "I don't know," she had shrugged absently, "do whatever you want. What difference does it make?"

The fear that none of it might make any difference remained my most troubling thought. My entrance into the church was my conscious statement that it did make a difference. But there was obviously more to me than my conscious side, and the other part of me had its own agenda. It took several years for these questions to be resolved.

The means of the resolution were strangely impersonal. I did not raise issues and discuss them. I didn't talk about these matters, whatever they were. What I did was endure, and go through the religious events of the year—Advent and Christmas and Lent and Easter—without consciously questioning their assumptions. I tried to celebrate Christmas and Easter, going to the services in our church and doing what I could at home. After several years it was no longer an effort, in fact it became a celebration anticipated with pleasure. My emotions fell in line with my mind. They ceased to sneak up on me, making their almost atavistic assault on my faith.

Since my baptism my sense of the church has changed. Before my baptism, and before my own confrontation with the limits of faith, I could take both faith and the church for granted. I had done so years before, during my first tour through the Renaissance cities of Italy. The church was just one of life's imperatives, like the buildings in New York or the communities of impoverished outside Mexico City—a physical presence with no moral dimensions. That's easy to do when you're an outsider looking at the church as one more part of life, an eternal institution powered by the spiritual struggles of others. But I can no longer afford that luxury. Now that it is a part of me I can see how dependent we are on each other.

I think that I can say with some accuracy that the person I am now and the person I was when I became a Catholic are rather different. I believe that I have changed as much since the day of my baptism as I did between the time of my initial conversion and my formal reception into the church. I do not want to speak of changing religiously, or to qualify these statements with a "religiously speaking," because this compartmentalization would not be accurate. It is I who have changed, not some part of me.

I recall that the priest who oversaw our entry into the church told us that the period after our reception, after all the ceremonies were completed and, to all intents and purposes, we became no different from any other Catholics, would be a critical phase of our conversion. He said that it is the time during which the ideas take root. They flourish or not depending on our willingness to take seriously our capacity and need for growth.

I was fortunate in that my reception into the church, as significant as it was, did not feel like a conclusion. It was only a stage in a process and I knew it. The process is life itself, and the conclusion is life's end. My life as a Catholic thus becomes an apprenticeship for this conclusion.

9

Sinfulness and Reconversion

Initiation into the life of the church neither presupposes nor brings about perfection, a fact that we mention for more than the obvious reasons. Nor is the sense of completion it conveys always continuing. The man or woman who enters the church by passing through the rites of initiation may have a sense that who and what I am has just been fully complemented. The decision stage of a conversion, as we noted earlier, can be euphoric. The entrance into a relationship with God, and the initiating community's frequently kind and open reception of the convert, especially when the community is as socially encompassing as the typical parish is today, can convey a strong sense of completion.

This initial sense is not illusory. But whatever its source it is more an image of our hopes, hopes grounded in and encouraged by our faith in what the future holds, than it is a picture of current reality. At the risk of sounding like the Scrooge of the Easter season I want to move from the joy that can be part of conversion to some of the negative areas that still remain as part of our lives afterward. The expansiveness that can so often be a mark of the convert is no more real than the limitation that is also a part of us. This limitation is not merely a diminution of our vision and choices. It is also a diminishing of our very desire for broader and better choices. It is the sinfulness that is part of who we are.

The new life of conversion is neither proof nor protection against this sinfulness. To the contrary, the realization of what salvation is all about can also become an instruction in the very meaning of sin. Earlier I spoke of sin as a wound, and the Christian life as a life of healing. Now I want to describe how the course of this healing runs through our lives. I also want to look at some of the other images that are used to describe both sin and its remedy, for I find that the combination of the theological, with its eminently rational method, and the poetic, with its own more intuitive approach, join together to form a much more penetrating view of the reality than either of them taken separately. The rite of initiation makes use of both, so we have a well-founded precedent for this approach.

The man or woman who has been through the church's rites of initiation has benefited from a strong and affirming passage. For many months, in some cases for several years, a substantial part of a community's efforts has gone to guide, strengthen, educate, and enlighten this person. But now the goal has been reached. The convert now takes his place among the church's full members. Initiation, however, is not yet complete. As the rite points out, "the time of postbaptismal catechesis is of great importance so that the neophytes, helped by their sponsors, may enter into a closer relationship with the faithful and bring them renewed vision and a new impetus." (Intro. 40) They are still on their pilgrimage, although they now travel as equals, both receiving from and giving to their new community.

This pilgrimage can be seen as a further healing of the sin that is part of us. Part of that healing is the awareness of its need. Our life together in the church not only instructs us in the nature of sin but also helps us see its presence in our life. With the confidence and optimism that ought to be a part of life we need not face this presence morosely nor let it get us down. For our faith should give us the desire and the means to remedy it, and the hope that it will be remedied.

Talk of sin and evil are somehow out of fashion today. This is strange, for the twentieth century has witnessed more than its share of both. Perhaps we have seen so much that a direct look at the evil in our world might threaten to overwhelm us. But to talk about conversion while ignoring our human capacity to create evil or to acquiesce before it, which is simply another way to speak of sin, is to miss one of the principal points of our faith.

Several images of human sinfulness stand out in my mind. I recall them because they are pictures of the ways that sin remains a part of our lives even after a conversion. They also help us to see how, in the process of resolving them, we can be brought to the need for a reconversion. In the early days of my ministry, during a year spent in Washington, D.C., I assisted one of the chaplains at the district prison with a discussion group for prisoners. For that year we met in the prison one night a week. On occasion we would talk about prison life. But as often as not the men wanted to talk about human issues having little to do with the grim reality of their imprisonment.

We met in a small, third-floor library next to an infrequently used stairs. The stairwell was concrete and the stairs themselves were made of steel. They led directly from a receiving entrance to a maximum security section. One evening during our session we heard several sirens wail in the distance, common enough in that part of Washington, but they began to command our attention as they drew near and it became clear how many there were. Immediately we heard the sound of car doors slamming outside. In a few moments shouts and curses echoed with an almost frantic pitch through the stairwell. Then a group of shackled men were hustled, one by one, up the staircase.

The men in our group fell totally silent. They sat looking nervously toward the open door at the end of the hall, saying nothing and moving hardly a muscle. The newly captured prisoners, big strong young men, were brought up the steel stairs and along the steel-floored corridor. The chains on their legs rang noisily as they banged from stair to stair and trailed behind them. Our direct view of them was limited to a fleeting glance as they passed the landing on our floor, but the drama of their arrival had made each second seem like minutes. Chained hand and foot, each one accompanied by several armed guards, they seemed the incarnation of violence and our own inadequate attempts to deal with it. Those images remain with me as pictures of moral failure drawn in human colors.

Each night as I left the prison, passing through the elaborate security system—first the two inner sets of bar doors one by one opening and then shutting behind me, then the solid steel door into the entrance corridor, finally the outer door that allowed me pass freely under the eye of the shotgun-carrying tower guard to my car—I would thank God that I did not have to spend a night in that place. How sorry I felt for the men inside. What a place to spend months, even years, of your life. No comprehending person who has heard the stories, or even the din, that come from such a place could think herself or himself unexposed to the fact of human evil.

Several years later, back in Berkeley, I worked with a few other teachers at the Graduate Theological Union interviewing soldiers from Fort Ord. The Vietnam War was at its height, and the military regulations permitted soldiers to file petitions seeking discharge as conscientious objectors. The petition process required that the authenticity of the soldier's change of heart since his induction be evaluated by a group of clergy. About a dozen of us agreed to spend our Sunday afternoons hearing the petitioners.

One young man came to see us, a conscripted Midwestern farm boy, the only child of a widowed mother. He was of marginal intelligence and struck me as being only slightly above the level of retardation. He seemed completely unaccustomed to coping with complexities and had great difficulty even in articulating his beliefs. It seemed to me that I spent hours helping him to put his ideas into a minimally orderly form.

With his limitations he was still good-hearted and almost guileless. As I spoke with him, painfully pulling out bits and pieces of ideas, it gradually became clear to me that he was a genuine pacifist and profoundly religious. He wanted to do what was right, and he felt called on to help his country. But he also thought that his faith and his duty were in conflict. In his simple biblical faith, expressed only with painful effort through the cloud of his own slowness, he thought he would be doing wrong if he hurt anyone for any reason. And by the end of our interview he had told me, almost with embarrassment, that he would lay down his life before he would shoot anyone.

But it took me several hours to get this information from him. On his chaplain's advice he was trying to take advantage of a process that required a mental sharpness and legal sophistication that were simply beyond him. There was no doubt in my mind that with his limitations he would soon be on a plane heading to Vietnam. In retrospect I think that had I been less concerned with my own sense of powerlessness than with the real obligations that the priesthood placed on me I would have been aggressive in my defense of his rights. These too, both the system that extends rights only to those strong enough to demand them and a moral sense immobilized by the sheer scope of moral issues, are pictures of sin.

Finally I think of a young man with whom I did some counseling. He was in his early thirties, and a professional. He had worked hard in college and graduate school, his eyes on the career in which he was now advancing rapidly, an advance that was very important to him. He also had married, and he and his wife had a five-year-old boy. I recall seeing them out bicycle-riding in one of our parks on a beautiful Sunday morning in May. The parents were riding ten-speed cycles, and the father, a good athlete who spent much of his spare time exercising, obviously wanted to pit his notable strength against the bicycle trail. The little boy, on a new balloon-tired two-wheeler, had struggled to keep up with them, had failed, and was now reduced to sobs and dejection as he trailed behind. The father was doing his best to pretend that he was alone, neither seeing nor hearing the ruckus behind him. The woman, both figuratively and literally, was halfway in between them, trying to keep the three together.

The man came to talk with me later on, and his state was no more than an elaboration of what I had seen in the park. Put simply, his wife and child were in the way. He had thought when he married that he would like being married and would like being a father. But if he ever enjoyed either he didn't like them now. His wife, his child, and his marriage were encroaching on his time and space. He was not getting from marriage what he wanted, and he wanted out. This view, which is common today, is also a picture of evil.

I recall these images because I think it is important for the convert to try to develop a sense of sin. One of the principal challenges facing the newly initiated Christian is the recognition of the ways in which evil is part of the fabric of his or her daily life. Prior to initiation the convert has had to come to terms with the more evident, personal sinfulness that we all have. But there are also more subtle injustices and violations that are part of our world, ones we take for granted because they are so pervasive and subtle. Part of our life's work is the attempt to bring correction where it is needed. And for this we need an understanding of what is evil, and why, and how this relates to our faith. This is what I mean by a sense of sin.

Today it is common for us to try to understand moral matters starting with the human condition rather than by starting with definitions of morality. We do this, I imagine, because we are more moved by our own concrete experiences than by ideas. And we are certainly not moved by notions of sin, especially the use of sin as a label. The extrinsic labeling of certain actions as sins, without some convincing rationale, is not only foreign to the Catholic tradition but also not very convincing today.

In past years sin was considered in different ways inside and outside the Catholic tradition. In the past, in the Catholic tradition, actions determined to be immoral using systems of religious ethics were gathered together in the category of sin. Outside the Catholic tradition religious leaders labeled actions sinful using biblical injunctions rather than a reference to the evil inherent in the action. Catholic morality, with its strong rational foundation, rejected this taboo-like use of sin. Rationales founded on scripture are quite different from condemnations quoting the scripture. And rationales developed to convince are different from condemnations designed to frighten and coerce.

But once again the arbitrary and extrinsic use of the notion of sin not only is with us but seems to be winning the day. We are living in an age of communication and entertainment. The word sin in the mouths of fundamentalist preachers, a use with dramatic frenzy and authoritarian insistence, is both entertaining and good copy. By comparison with full-blown fanaticism the arguments of ethics seem dull.

So, in defense or as a result, in our Catholic context we discuss sin not as such but within its human context, as I did above. It has not always been so. For the medievals sin was a common topic, the subject of art, of symbols, and of theological definitions. Their view of sin was less personal and more transcendent. For them the principal discussions of sin involved such subjects as the disobedience of Adam and Eve and their expulsion from paradise. As the artwork from the times indicates, this was a common topic of religious education. So was the fall of the angels from paradise. Thomas Aquinas, in discussing the latter, defined sin as the desire for singularity in excellence. But this kind of discussion, obviously definitional and of great interest to them, is of much less interest today.

There are those, I know, who define evil as a problem. Ah, yes, they say, the problem of evil. To me that makes it sound like the recollection of some event from an irrelevant past, like Henry Wallace's run for the presidency. I admit that I am wary of those who speak of evil and pain as problems. I recall a sermon I heard on what the preacher called the problem of suffering. And as he talked I recall thinking to myself, "I don't think this man has ever had so much as a toothache." Evil is not a problem, for problems can be solved. Evil is a reality. It is something we live with. Perhaps we live with it exercising some control, and perhaps we have no control. But in either case we live with it because it is so prevalent in our world.

Our lives develop their moral quality through the way we respond to evil. There is evil in the world around us, and there is evil in us. And the way we choose to live with this evil, it seems to me, becomes one of the principal means we use to give to our lives their moral quality. Both individually and collectively we are called on to free ourselves and one another from the evils that are part of us and of our lives. How we respond to that call reflects our current moral state and brings our future moral selves into being.

Living morally requires that, from the beginning, we recognize evil for what it is. But this recognition is not all that easy. In the process of developing our sense of sin and evil we can find that we have a greater need of definitions and ideas than is commonly available today. For our own humanistically oriented sense of sin, which is pictured above in the examples I gave and in which I share, proves to be too narrow. With our experience as the starting point of our questions and answers, and our experience colored by the desire for comfort and complementary isolation that is built into American life, we find that issues coming from outside this context can get no hearing.

Discovering the meaning and existence of evil in our world requires that we become open to questions other than our own. Why is liberation so important an issue in Latin America? Why are church leaders in Eastern Europe, on the other hand, so concerned about personal morality? Why are questions of social justice raised so often by the American bishops? These questions, except for the last, may not be our questions, for they come from contexts other than our own. And they look at moral issues from a public point of view, rather than the individual viewpoint which is common in America.

It is also possible that the convert really does not have many questions. The process of initiation can be experienced as not only personally supportive but intellectually reassuring as well. I am not sure that this reassurance is all that positive. The pilgrimage that reaches its public high point in the rite of initiation is not meant to lull the convert into a moral sleep. Rather it is to sharpen the wit as well as strengthen the will for what is ahead. And what is ahead is a life of continuous moral growth.

Going beyond the common and the cultural is essential to moral growth. Converts who hope to deepen their appreciation of their new faith have to be prepared to see things in a new way, even to the point of saying that my moral state at the time of my initiation into the church was incomplete. It means being willing to examine our attitudes to our faith and church to see where they are in need of refining. And it probably means the willingness to develop some of the intellectual tools to equip us for these tasks.

In retrospect I can see that at the time of my ordination my attitude toward the institutions of ministry was as much determined by my own needs as by the pastoral purpose of those institutions. It was only in the course of my clinical training, which began three years after my ordination, that I was able to see clearly the limitations in my views of ministry. I was limited by what, with kindness to myself, I can call a lack of experience, and by what, with more accuracy, I can call a lack of generosity.

I was also genuinely limited by the want of an intellectual framework that could explain service in functional rather than moral terms. I had been given many talks telling me to be of service, but very few lessons, if any, explaining how. I was helped to grow beyond this point by a clinical training program specifically designed to provide this help, among other things. The training group was supportive and highly intelligent. My supervisors pinpointed my strengths in a way that mobilized my confidence.

In addition, I was looking for and found a rationale that made service intelligible. It seems ironic that the most convincing rationale for my ministry came from a clinical, not a religious, source. But heretofore I had been given religious and poetic reasons that seemed to miss the point. The poetic reasons spoke of the joys of sacrifice and rang no more true than generals' praise of privates' front-line heroism. And the religious reasons missed the excitement and challenge of work.

The view that seemed to function in our clinic, and which we articulated more informally than formally, was that our work was fascinating and involving but in the long run very draining. To justify this effort we had to have a set of values that placed the well-being of the people we were serving above our own well-being. And we all recognized that, ultimately, we had to look within ourselves for the source of this altruism. This meant calling on our own spiritual resources and developing them where the call found them wanting. Our group was about evenly divided between Christians and Jews, and most were both believing and practicing. So in one another we found a real stimulus to developing personal resources for institutional work.

I mention this because I believe that our situation was analogous to that of the convert who is developing his or her own spiritual resources. On the one hand there is probably a sense of respect, in fact probably something much deeper than respect, for the church as an institution. There may well be a trust that runs very deep, because this institution has recently provided the rite that has been the means for the conversion's taking its effect. And the church has provided this not just as a collection of individuals but as an organic body, the source of whose unity is its most animating principle. For this reason the human wisdom and divine spark that are written into the very motions of the rite are convincing.

On the other hand there can be a pull toward a personalization of faith and the development of a sense that says that moral responsibility is ultimately individual. The decision about what is right and wrong is essentially a single, not a collective, decision. And, in difficult matters, it can be arrived at by a process that proves to be as lonely as it is, on occasion, isolating.

The institution has been like a parent, and the rite uses imagery drawn from the nourishing aspect of family life. It has fanned the spark of the new life and has provided the means for growth. It can and should continue to be a source of nourishment and direction. And yet in the area of concrete, moral choices the adult has to grow beyond dependence on an institution. In the area of moral priorities the individual has to bring a critical eye to bear on institutional priorities. For communities can become languid and, in their need to deal with disruptive forces, repressive. Just as each individual has to establish him or herself as a distinct person separate from his or her family, something that in no way reflects negatively on either, so the convert should grow beyond the kind of trust in which the critical sense is not that of an adult. Put simply, the adult convert has to become morally critical and discerning.

I have found that in one way this process has enhanced my own appreciation of institutions, and in another indicated the deep need for a well-developed, individual conscience. The institution, especially in its rituals, has the ability to move us. Symbols still seem to maintain their power to affect. They are especially useful in transmitting traditional authority structures. The sacramental rituals of holy orders and matrimony create a new generation of church and family institutions with an economy of means almost unmatched in civil society.

Yet we are left with the need to judge institutional priorities and values. That we feel moved, or that we feel anything at all, is no basis for moral action. For that we need reasonable principles, and the intellectual effort required in their thoughtful application.

We can resist the need to use principles just as we can resist the move toward the isolation that can be the lot of the moral man or woman. We can prefer the camaraderie of the agreeable. But in this we are, I believe, acquiescing to the evil that is in the world. We are settling for the comfort of group thought. I am just old enough to remember the newsreels of the Madison Square Garden rally of the German-American Bund, a pro-Nazi group, on Washington's Birthday in 1939. Even then, as a small child, I was impressed by how triumphantly happy all the participants seemed to be. I have seen this same euphoric glow on the faces of recent fundamentalist converts. All questions answered, all doubts resolved, all hesitations now recast in the bronze of collective certainty. For me it is a terribly frightening prospect, and very far from the Catholic tradition.

In our move into the days beyond sacramental initiation we can anticipate that the essential limitation of human knowledge, and the darkness of faith, will raise questions. These questions can be serious, and their answers unsettling. I recall that my religious formation and education for the priesthood in no way anticipated the kind of ministry that seemed almost to come tumbling upon the American church after the Vatican Council and during the civil rights movement and the Vietnam War. These events raised questions about institutions, about authority, and about obedience that I never expected I would have to answer. By the time the dust of these years' turmoil had begun to settle, three quarters of my classmates and most of my friends had left the priesthood and the church. The human context of my adult religious life simply disappeared. For a man whose faith is written in human lines that loss felt devastating.

Such times can bring us, once again, to a point in our lives where we recognize that things have got to change. We approach the turn in our road this time enlivened by a faith, and this time as members of a believing community, but the turn in the road is still a turning point. We approach it often with our weaknesses struggling again to reassert themselves. There is the willingness to settle for less, the fatigue or boredom with God and his ways, the desire to coast rather than walk uphill. In my case these attitudes were all supported by a chorus of reflected voices, aspects of my self, that told me what one side wanted to hear. The fact of choice is as real and as disconcerting as its need.

These are the times of conversion, and of reconversion. They are real, and they continue to be part of us. The man or woman who has been initiated into the life of the church can anticipate that this life will retain its dynamic of choice, and its need for choice. For choice and sinfulness and conversion to good or evil are a part of who we are.

10

Truths and The Truth:
The Role of Theology

Conversion is a process, but it is more than a process. It is an ongoing process. For this reason we can speak of the conversions in our life, recognizing that the process may well involve several turning points, each one a genuine conversion. The fact that a person has been formally and publicly initiated into the church does not mean that growth, change, and even change to the point of conversion, are over. The deepening of our understanding of what it is that has happened to us cannot help but work its effect.

Over the centuries the church's theological tradition has been concerned principally with truth and unchanging reality. As soon as we begin to speak of a search for truth we can seem to move out of the concrete world in which we live into an abstract and unchanging world, a world of scholars and philosophers rather than a world of ordinary people. And it may seem that much of our theology is firmly fixed in this abstract world.

But the church's theological tradition is not so one-sided. It also recognizes the reality of change in human affairs. To bridge what otherwise might be a gap between our human lives, in all their transience, and truth in all its abstract purity, the theology makes a distinction between The Truth and our own individual truths. The one exists as an abstract and inclusive concept. Our truths, on the other hand, are the single, limited realizations about ourselves and our world that come to us in the course of our lives. For all their limitation our truths are nonetheless genuinely true. They are also the object of theological study.

One of the most fundamental principles in Catholic theology is the realization that we discover The Truth only bit by bit, never in one complete, all-encompassing view. Our views of what is true are always partial. What we know may be quite true, but it is never the whole truth. We may have our eyes well focused on some aspect of The Truth, but there is always going to be another aspect behind our backs. And so we can never claim to have a monopoly on truth. In this final chapter I want to describe a way we can relate The Truth, in all its permanence and unchangeability, to the fact of change, growth, and conversion in our lives.

We begin with the fact that our knowledge, by its very nature, is limited. This can be a disconcerting fact, for it is humbling to admit that something we know may be quite true but insignificant compared with other truths. I, for one, found it humbling. Like many a young man I was not so much intent on learning the truth as on imposing it. Studies for me were not a search but a contest. The male ego, it seems, wants order. And the youthful ego wants to dominate. At least it was so with me. That combination, which adds up to ignorance in action, can be as fearsome as it is potent.

I suspect that the appeal to youth of so many right-wing nationalist movements in the first half of the twentieth century, and of left-wing internationalist movements in the second half, is that they provide a natural home for the adolescent contest with truth. They provide membership in a self-assured and vital group that claims to have a corner on the truth. From their home in the order of mind, where conclusions can follow easily from premises, rather than the order of concrete reality with its irksome need to make things work, they can suggest their own historical inevitability. This, in turn, gives them justification for treating lightly the civil and individual rights of others, which stand in the way of what simply must come to be.

Religious groups can make the same appeal if they claim to have a corner on the truth. Using some rather bad logic, Christians have been guilty of this in the past. They have said that God is Truth, that we know God with the certitude of faith, and therefore we know The Truth with that same certitude. It won't sell. For we know God not in God's way, which is infinite, but in our way, which is limited. Any concern for truth requires that we recognize how partial and limited are our human views of truth. This is especially important for the convert, for we need to approach the future not closed off to its lessons but recognizing that we still have much to learn.

I was fortunate in that I was introduced to theology by teachers who explained very clearly the limitations of human knowing. At that time in the Dominican Order our study of theology followed the method used by St. Thomas Aquinas, and he was a master in explaining the limits of knowledge. Questions of method were given a major emphasis. Why a creative genius works the way he or she does was presented to us as a question just as worth knowing about as the product of that creativity. We studied not only the content of ideas, but equally the very meaning of ideas and knowing. This led inevitably to a study of nineteenth- and twentieth-century ideas on the process of knowing.

Several principles found in the works of St. Thomas promoted that thoughtful approach. One is the idea I have been discussing: the realization that while truth, in itself, may be one, the mind knows only truths. Our most synthetic, overarching theory can be at most a partial view. And that partial picture seems inevitably bound to come up against another, sooner or later, that will describe the subject in a fuller and better way. Our human intellect is limited by its very nature to a series of partial though true views which we analyze and synthesize as best we can, knowing that we will never have a full view of the truth.

For the intellectually ambitious young man, these ideas can sound defeatist. What is the purpose in trying to construct the perfect world system if your starting theory says the task is impossible? So the political idealists have had to abandon these limiting theories in favor of utopian views. The Hegelian system used by Marx, for example, skirts this limitation by introducing a belief in a future fulfillment, called the historical process. If you can't bring about perfection today you can at least be part of the historical process that moves, program by program or synthesis by synthesis, to that utopia. No doubt this is one reason that Marxism has its appeal to young intellectuals intent on rebuilding the world.

But there is more to theology than this attempt to get at The Truth. This philosophical view of truth is not the only view. Theology also attempts to discover truth by trying to answer life's questions. I was fortunate in that my very first lecture in theology was used to make this point, a point I have never forgotten.

The lecturer was one of the leading theologians in the country, and a man of unusual wisdom. At the very beginning of the opening lecture of the year, during which we were scheduled to study questions of human choice, he began to pace back and forth before us, apparently pondering what he anticipated was our principal question: why. Why study something so abstract, so formal, and so ancient in this day and age? He walked for a while, obviously thinking, and then turned to us. "In a professional school," he began with no words of introduction, "you teach the students the skills of that profession. You give them enough knowledge, and develop sufficient skills, so that they can go about their work with competence and confidence. And there are those who look at education for the priesthood in much the same light. But here we are really trying to do something quite different," he said as he turned to us. "We are teaching you the theology of the church," he said, using his index finger to drum out the emphases he was making, "so that you can make sense of your lives. And then," he added reflectively after a moment's pause, "having learned to do so for yourselves, you may be able to help others do the same."

Almost instinctively, it seemed, I knew what he was talking about. I was sitting in that room not because I wanted to become an ecclesiastical technician but because I wanted to make sense of my life. I learned, later on, that the highest points in the church's theological development were reached, for the same reason, during periods of reform. The church's theological leaders, from Augustine and Aquinas to John of the Cross and the theologians of Vatican II, developed their theological ideas not to no end but as rationales for their reforms.

For this reason the theologian has to have an effective involvement in the issues that place life's questions in focus. For me Berkeley's countercultural viewpoint served to raise questions, but that same countercultural uniformity led not to real questions and answers but to a kind of offbeat conformity. My first regular pastoral work, on the other hand, was a whirlwind of social involvement. It raised questions that required that I really stretch my mind, and it set me in the very middle of a turmoil that called on all my human strengths in order to cope with it.

I completed my theological studies in Washington, D.C., in June of 1964. The very day after I returned to California I was asked to work on the staff of a program in human relations for about one hundred and fifty high school students. The program, sponsored by the National Conference of Christians and Jews, was scheduled to begin in forty-eight hours at a camp in the mountains outside Los Angeles, and the priest on the staff had fallen ill. The program was too complex to explain by phone, I was told, but it would all be explained on my arrival in Los Angeles.

After I arrived it became clear that they had kept me in the dark because they didn't want to scare me away. The program was involving and challenging. The students, I was told, would be drawn from very different backgrounds—white, black, Hispanic, Asian, poor, and rich, and from all religious backgrounds as well as from none. Many would be older, wise in the ways of the streets if not of the world, articulate, and able. We should anticipate real antagonism among the diverse groups, but, the antipathies notwithstanding, we were to try to give them an experience of community. On Monday I had defended a dissertation on an abstract point of moral theology. On Saturday I was on my way into a social maelstrom.

These were days of turmoil. Just seven months previously President Kennedy had been assassinated. During the days of our program three civil rights workers were murdered in Mississippi. The news of their disappearance was very troubling to the youngsters, who were still feeling the effects of the assassination. They had been recruited because of their leadership ability in their respective communities. The white students were believers in the value of public leadership. The non-white were becoming skilled practitioners of effective confrontation. They came from Watts and Compton, from Bel Air and Beverly Hills, and they were becoming aware that these communities and their institutions were examples of the same divisions that the headlines were associating with the South.

All of the students were being overtaken by more change than any of us had as yet had to cope with. Because the clergy were playing such visible roles in the civil rights movement, most of them were turning to us for answers. The course of events had wrenched the lid from the pot, and we were expected to make sense of what now was boiling up and over.

Initially I felt woefully unprepared for this effort. My theological education had been principally in the area of definitions, and I had little training in public leadership. But as the yellow school busses, one after the other, rolled noisily into camp and their young passengers climbed down and formed themselves into separate, tight, and self-defensive racial groups, the limits of my education became quite irrelevant. I had signed onto a staff that was expected to produce. The first lesson of leadership maintains that when you are in charge only your actions count, not your excuses. And we were in charge. So it was up to us to help these youngsters make sense of what they were going through.

Word of the disappearances and suspected murders in Mississippi caused events in the program, which had taken on all the agenda of the civil rights movement, to move faster than the planners had anticipated. Pent-up resentments began to burst out, fears and guilt began to immobilize, group antipathies were finding human faces, and we had to make sense of it all.

This was no time for hand-wringing. The truth was that we were the leaders by our own choice. It was our program. We were supposed to know how to articulate questions and develop answers, and we had best recall how to do it. My own values and the public vocation I had espoused were also being put to the test in what was proving to be the most difficult social question our country has had to face. And in the event that I might have missed the point there was an army of youngsters who wanted me to relate my faith, my vocation, and myself to the issues. Questions of truth seemed almost irrelevant in this context of emotion and concrete need. Yet what we were searching for was truths of the deepest order.

There was no doubt in my mind about the appropriateness of being involved in this work. Seven years earlier I had come to California to enter the Dominicans because of the example of integrity in a time of crisis on the part of the Dominican provincial superior. He had come from California and had made a well-publicized tour of the French Dominican provinces at a time when they were under fire for spearheading the programs of church reform that led to Vatican II. His support of the Dominicans, who were playing such a central role in my own life, led to my decision to enter the order in California. It also strengthened my attitude toward the place of integrity in the life of the church. My New Jersey roots were too well set in the realities of political expediency to expect integrity at every turn, but seeing it surface at these critical times reinforced my belief that it really represented the way things ought to be.

This same man had also taken a strong and symbolic stand in support of academic freedom. During the McCarthy era the University of California had required a loyalty oath of its faculty. Eleven professors refused to sign it and were removed from teaching. The United States Supreme Court subsequently declared the oath unconstitutional and ordered their reinstatement. But prior to that reinstatement he invited one of the suspended professors, a renowned medievalist, to deliver a public lecture in our house of studies in Oakland. Since our house was only minutes away from the campus, the invitation had the effect of offering the scholar a public forum immediately adjacent to the university. In the climate of the times the invitation was a courageous act.

In retrospect I see these as instances of moral truth surfacing in human affairs. And I see my own introduction to the ministry equally as an example of the way in which we can be brought face-to-face with the need for truth. The truths that surfaced were limited. They were focused only on a particular problem in a particular cultural setting. But they surfaced in a way which fully involved me. Not only did this surfacing involve me, it mobilized me.

Religious formation, like most socialization I imagine, seeks to bend the initiate to the needs of the socializing institution. And the men who ran our institutions at that time thought they needed priests who could be moved about at will, rather than be aggressive in arranging their ministries themselves. This first formal ministry, following upon the limited work I had done with the people who came to our seminary chapel, made me depend on my own resources. It mobilized my creativity and in the process it liberated me from any romantic notion I might have had that someone else would, or could, direct my work for me. Jesus told his followers to know the truth, and the truth would make them free. Through my own moving encounter with some of the painful truths of American life I found myself freed from a dependence on institutional cues for my own actions. I was learning that only I could bring the relevant principles to bear on actions for which I was responsible. This, too, was an instance of a truth surfacing in the concrete. For the convert learning to integrate the role of church authority into his or her life this can be a valuable if difficult lesson.

A few months later, with the Vatican Council in full swing, I became involved in what eventually proved to be a successful attempt to establish a Catholic community at the Graduate Theological Union in Berkeley. Our efforts were not universally applauded, even less understood. So before my first year of ministry was half over I was told to go away and study for two years. And if I couldn't study I should at least go away. Since the final date for school applications was long since past I suspected that the latter half of the message was the more important.

Fortunately, even at that late date I was able to secure a fellowship for a pilot program in clinical training sponsored by the National Institute of Mental Health. The following September I was in Philadelphia, at the University of Pennsylvania's medical school. I was to be trained as a counselor in a family study unit of the psychiatric department.

Here, too, truths surfaced, truths of a very different kind. They were truths about human motivations, about human capacities in both common and stressful situations, and truths about the way people relate to one another. Once again they were limited, but they were liberating. Their difference in style from the religious truths I had become familiar with, and these from the ministerial truths, supported my impression that our human knowledge of ultimate truth is a patchwork of unlikely pieces.

In these first months and years of my ministry I was exposed, in many cases against my will and with no planning on my part, to situations that brought me face to face with the need for truth. I had to face the fact that things were frequently not the way I had thought them to be. But I was not content simply to leave it at that. I wanted to understand how they really were, and to find some thread of connection between them.

Needless to say, I was not alone in this. The entire church was attempting to cope with the destruction of the war years, the mobility that followed, and the change in the intellectual systems in which it defined its life. We were all learning, and, most important, we were learning in and from the mobility that was part of our life. This had an effect on the way we came to understand our theology, because we recognized that our theologizing did not take place in a state of freedom from the environment, as in a kind of mental laboratory.

Much of pre-Vatican II theology, to the contrary, saw the theological process as essentially a laboratory effort, a study that took place free from the limiting conditions that are part of life. Like laboratory science, it was analytic and reductionist. It saw the church, like the world, the human psyche, and all things, as made of a finite number of constituent parts, like the atoms of the physical world or the id and ego of the psychic world.

The bishops of the Vatican Council changed that view. They came up with a more synthetic view that was less dependent on the analytic sciences of the nineteenth century. The method they pioneered is now known as systems theory. And the definition of the church that came out of the Council is a prime, if coincidental, example of systems theory put to work. Interestingly enough, Thomas Aquinas had taught that the reason our knowledge of truth is always limited is that the human mind proceeds, as he wrote, *componendo et dividendo,* by synthesizing and analyzing. The theological conservatives who opposed these new views, some of whom had cut their intellectual teeth as schoolboys excelling in the physics lab, were strong proponents both of his ideas and of the analytic method. But in their analytic view of the church they overlooked the other half of Aquinas's methodology, the role of synthesis in our knowing.

That these times of turmoil were the occasion for such major theological development points up another facet of Catholic theology. Like the life of the church, it is social. It has come out of a community and it is principally for a community. In our eminently individualistic age it is easy to overlook the social role of religion, of Christian living, and of theology. Yet in the Catholic tradition this social role is a very important one, and today it serves as one of the principal countercultural and prophetic aspects of the church's life.

As I began my ministry I needed to have this social dimension reinforced, for it had not been a central part of my formation. I did not really trust the subjective and individualist approach of our formation, but I had yet to have the kind of pastoral experience that would provide an alternative. I have already discussed my venture into Jungian record-keeping. Looking back I think that I was really bored by these effete, anti-intellectual games. They were entertaining during the student years of powerlessness, but the appeal of the subjective pales in the face of concrete opportunity. Even more, I think I was truly suspicious of the subjective. Our grasp of truth might be partial, but it is objective. What is true is true. How you feel about it or what the knowledge does for you in no way changes the fact of that truth.

One way in which the subjective gains a foothold today in theology is through its presentation as being spiritual. We can be given the impression that there are religious truths, subjective in nature, that are somehow different, special, even more true. And they are more true because they are more spiritual.

On occasion I have used the words spiritual and spirituality, and I know they are used frequently in religious writings. I want to qualify my use of these words because I find that their use is often confusing. I have heard religious writers speak of doing things for the right spiritual reasons. And it can sound as though spiritual reasons are not only better reasons but somehow quite different from the reasons that motivate ordinary mortals.

When I was young one of the local pastors had the reputation for being very spiritual. Parishioners' questions, which in those days usually had to do with surviving the Depression, were met with spiritual answers. That meant they were answers no one could quite manage to connect with the question. And, as a cynical uncle described it, they were delivered with the trusting smile of a Republican peeking around the corner for prosperity.

The man's trust was apparently not vindicated and it was more than he could handle. He ended up in the state hospital. My uncle described the news as it was brought to him by an employee who approached life, and the English language, in a state of wonder. "Did you hear the news! The revenue, he's gone daft. They took him away. Carried him out in his office chair they did, still gazin' into space."

The occasionally spacey quality of spiritual matters is not a new phenomenon. It was actually one of the principal issues debated in the Middle Ages, another aspect of the relationship between the sacred and the secular. And the debate helped clarify the nature of theology as well as the limits to the use of the word spiritual.

The issue faced by the theologians was the desire to come up with a unified theology. They wanted a means to connect all the issues they were discussing, to weave them together into a coherent whole, and know that the connection was valid. They were faced with terribly disruptive social situations that came from looking at questions of law and justice from two competing points of view, the spiritual and the nonspiritual. They wanted to avoid a dualism in matters of truth (and a parallel dualism in matters of political authority), with one truth for the spiritual, another for the nonspiritual.

The principal medieval theologians proposed a theory that unified theology. Theology, they said, had only one subject—God. It saw God first in himself, then God as the author of creation, and then God as the goal of all creatures. All life was seen as coming from God and returning to God. Our human life was seen as a pilgrimage from God and back to God. The church and the sacraments and the Christian life were the means used for this return to God.

With this unified view there was no need to speak of moral theology and biblical theology and spiritual theology. There was only theology, a study of God into which all things could be placed in a rational and orderly way. The parceling of theology into different, noncontinuous disciplines is a departure from this tradition. Historically it has been the sign of a low point in theological study. It is the sign of a shift from science to technique. We live with it today because there is no science that encompasses human knowledge sufficiently to form the basis for an equally encompassing theology. The nineteenth century's confidence in a science that would both enumerate and order all that could be known, and that led to an equally confident theology, is simply no longer possible. Today we believe that our ability to measure and explain will never be commensurate with our ability to observe what is there.

Consequently we have not a theology but theologies. We know that this plurality is the sign of our own limitations. It is a mirror held up to the divisions inherent not only in our world but in our ways of thinking as well. Wisdom would call us to see the lesson of humility implicit in this fact, and approach truth knowing that it is larger than our ability to comprehend. The course of our life is marked by days each of which is too finite to follow the tracings of God's hand in that day alone. But these limitations notwithstanding, the truths we learn are truly learned. The signs of God are truly seen. And that is cause for hope.

In the course of life the convert has seen how the truths that once explained life somehow became inadequate. Questions arose whose answers could not be found within categories that, to that point, had served quite well. As a result the former truths, the functioning answers, and the systems that supported each of these came into question. Through the sometimes painful process of change and searching, new answers were reached—answers that involved a turning in life itself. A conversion took place.

Throughout this book we have looked at the characteristics that commonly mark the process of conversion. Our context has been the church's ritual for the initiation of adult members. Ritual seeks to form rather than instruct, and is not explanatory. We have attempted to compensate for the nonexplanatory nature of ritual by explaining both conversion and initiation.

That ritual is fixed is obvious. This set quality is both intentional and essential. But if there is any quality that is to be encouraged in the converts themselves, it is an openness to life and its lessons. The Greek word mystagogia, which is used to characterize the period after the formal initiation, refers to a growth in the truths that life presents to us. This presentation may be a confrontation or it may be a gentle lesson. We have seen examples of each. Whatever form it may take, it is a benefit to us because it brings us face to face with that for which we are made.